Lectures on Jung's *Aion*

polarities of the psyche

A series edited by Emmanuel Kennedy-Xypolitas

Lectures on Jung's *Aion*

Barbara Hannah
Marie-Louise von Franz

Chiron Publications
Wilmette, Illinois

Second Printing 2008

Book and cover design by Peter Altenberg.
Printed in the United States of America.

Library of Congress Cataloging-in-Publication Data

Lectures on Jung's Aion / Barbara Hannah, Marie-Louise von Franz.
p. cm. -- (Polarities of the Psyche)
Includes bibliographical references and index.
ISBN 10: 1-888602-28-7 ISBN 13: 978-1-888602-28-9
1. Jung, C. G. (Carl Gustav), 1875-1961. Aion. 2. Self. 3. Psychology, Religious. I. Hannah, Barbara. Process of individuation in Aion. II. Franz, Marie-Louise von, 1915- Conversations on Aion. III. Series.
BF175.5.S44J8635 2004
150.19 54--dc22
2004005673

"There is nothing in nature
that does not contain as much
evil as good."

—Gerhard Dorn

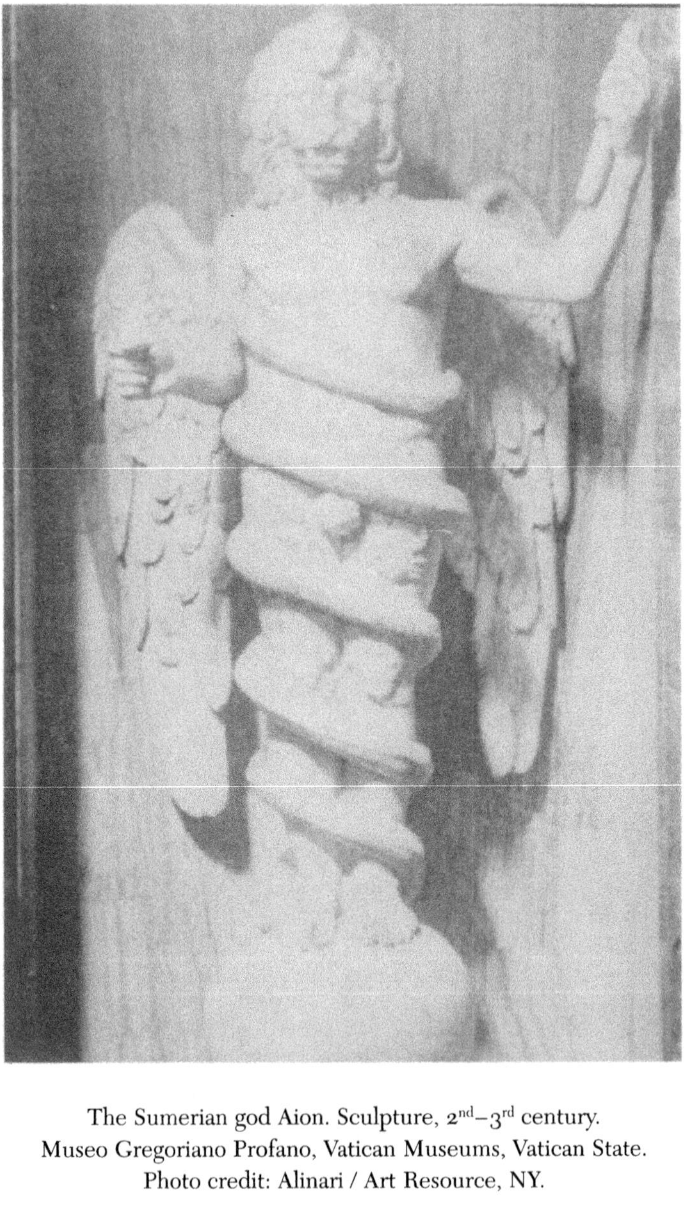

The Sumerian god Aion. Sculpture, 2nd–3rd century.
Museo Gregoriano Profano, Vatican Museums, Vatican State.
Photo credit: Alinari / Art Resource, NY.

Contents

Editor's Note

THE FOCUS OF THE SERIES POLARITIES OF THE PSYCHE is the broad theme of the opposites in the psyche, which are, according to the great Swiss psychiatrist Carl Gustav Jung, the basis of every life process.

This is the first of several volumes that will include lectures by Barbara Hannah, who was both a pupil and close friend of C. G. Jung. Apart from Jung himself, there may be no other Jungian analyst who was more concerned with the opposites in human nature than Barbara Hannah. I believe her great interest in this topic came about because it was her own fate to deal with the inner opposites *consciously*, a fate revealed to her by the unconscious.

Throughout her childhood, Barbara Hannah had two recurring dreams, or, to put it more precisely, two aspects of one dream. She was so frightened by the dream, especially the second aspect, that she was sometimes afraid to go to sleep for fear of experiencing it again.

In the first and most frequent version of the dream, she was standing by the open doors to the House of Commons in London. A revolution was going on outside in which people were killing each other, just as they had done in the French Revolution. It was said in the dream that if she went out unarmed, the revolution would stop of its own accord. The dream always ended with Barbara Hannah trying to gather up the courage to do so.

In the other, more alarming aspect of the dream, she was in a small pony carriage and she was being taken to be hung – a further parallel to the French Revolution. The carriage passed through a dense crowd of people, and she never knew if they felt hostile or friendly towards her.

Barbara Hannah never forgot this dream, but she had not the slightest idea what it meant until she told the two aspects to Jung shortly after beginning her analysis with him when she was thirty-nine years old. Jung said that the dream was a forecast of her whole life: *it was her fate to face the opposites*. If she did so willingly – that is, if she walked out into the fight as helplessly as a child might do – it would end positively, the opposites would be reconciled to each other. But if she refused, she would still be forced to hang between the opposites, and it would end negatively.

Subsequent dreams brought the problem of the opposites – especially the problem of good and evil – into Barbara Hannah's everyday life, and she was confronted with a lifelong task. One could say it was her fate to follow the will of the Self, of that higher inner polarity superordinate to the ego. She once said, "I realized that the *hieros gamos* (sacred marriage) and somehow uniting those opposites was my myth and that my whole fate in the Infinite depended on my somehow fulfilling it. Indeed it might be much more than a personal matter, its fulfillment might even lay a grain on the scales of fate: the two possibilities of the opposites clashing in atomic war or finding each other in the *hieros gamos*."

The Polarities of the Psyche series includes lectures of Barbara Hannah on the problem of the psychic opposites in both the personal and in the transpersonal, that is, archetypal realm. For the most part, these lectures were held at the Psychological Club and at the C. G. Jung Institute in Zürich, where she lectured until her death. The lectures cover almost the entire spectrum of analytical psychology. They deal with basic human experiences of, for example, the personal and collective unconscious, the shadow, the animus and anima, the Self, good and evil, possession, the confrontation with and the integration of the unconscious, individuation or realization of the Self, the God-image, and finally the experience of the Godhead.

Barbara Hannah's lectures were always well attended and highly appreciated. Both the lectures of Marie-Louise von Franz, who was Barbara Hannah's lifelong friend, and Barbara Hannah's own lectures comprised a major contribution to the training at the Jung Institute, for they conveyed a true feeling of Jung's living psychology. Even today there are those whose recollection of these lectures is still vivid. Many have expressed the wish to have access to the lectures in some form, a wish that makes apparent the genuine need of laypeople, of trainees, and of analysts to have a taste, as it were, of the spirit embodied in Jung's life and work, which both women were able to experience directly.

What makes Barbara Hannah's writings so valuable is that they spring out of real experience of the depths of the psyche, which is also the *Numen*. It is this direct experience of the unconscious in her writings and life that she shares so completely with Jung.

The present volume deals with Jung's book *Aion*, in which he outlines the course of Western history as revealed in the gradual development of archetypal constellations in the collective unconscious. In the five lectures that make up part I, which were held at the C. G. Jung Institute in Zürich in 1957, Barbara Hannah discusses the essential points made in Jung's book.

Also included here is an interview with Marie-Louise von Franz, "Conversations on *Aion*." This two-hour interview took place in the spring of 1965 at her home in Küsnacht. Concerning the interview, Claude Drey, the interviewer, writes:

> At the time there were a great many questions I wanted to find answers to with regard to *Aion* by C. G. Jung. Due to the short time available, I had to limit myself to a few questions on

> the book's last chapter, "The Structure and Dynamics of the Self" ... The conversation was written up so others too might benefit from this type of effort to clarify some sentences in this chapter which for me presented difficulties in understanding.

The quotations in this present volume have been taken from R. F. C. Hull's translations in the Bollingen Series XX, *The Collected Works of C. G. Jung*, volume 9ii, published by Pantheon Books in 1959 and reprinted in 1969 by Princeton University Press.[1] This volume of Jung's *Collected Works* does not include the contribution of his co-worker, Marie-Louise von Franz, "Die Passio Perpetuae," from the first Swiss edition, volume VII of the *Psychologische Abhandlungen, 8* – a contribution included by Jung himself. Hannah refers to it in her introduction.

Barbara Hannah was renowned for her simple, feminine, introverted wisdom. Marie-Louise von Franz was renowned for her unique creative spirit. Each in her own way brings one of Jung's most difficult and complete works to life and conveys the essence and spirit of Jungian psychology.[2]

1. In her original lecture notes, Barbara Hannah thanks R. F. C. Hull for having allowed her access to a first draft of his translation of *Aion*, but she warns the listener (reader) not to quote from it, as it was "by no means the final version."
2. See also the excellent book by Edward F. Edinger: *The Aion Lectures: Exploring the Self in C. G. Jung's Aion*, edited by Deborah A. Wesley (Toronto: Inner City Books, 1996).

The Process of Individuation in *Aion*

Barbara Hannah

Introduction

LAZY PEOPLE TAKE THE MOST PAINS! I CHOSE *Aion* from a number of themes offered me, because I had given it before, but soon saw that lectures before a book is published and after are something totally different.[1] Therefore I decided – except for a few pages of the introduction – to start again and redo it from A to Z. I shall read next to nothing from the book this time and instead have prepared a short summary in my own words of each chapter, but I wish to emphasize that this in no way replaces reading the book.[2] This is not a star course so I cannot oblige you to work outside the lectures, but I think the discussion would benefit enormously if you were to read the next piece and prepare any questions you want to ask or comments you want to make.

I propose, therefore, before we start discussing each chapter, to first read my summary, in which I attempt only to extract the main line – rather like a line of cats' eyes put down to keep the cars from losing the road – and then to ask you one or two questions or make some comment of my own, formulated with the purpose of getting the discussion started, because I am sure, in the case of a difficult book like *Aion*, that it can only be understood through discussion.

One thing I should like to make clear from the beginning is that in condensing – I have used perhaps ten words where Jung has used thousands – I have sometimes put things much more brutally and frankly than Jung himself has done. I am well aware that the whole book *Aion* is very much more tactful than I have been. As I said before, I have only tried to bring out the main line and if at times I have thus been too blunt and it offends you, please blame me and not Jung, for he has often used pages to lead up to and explain a conclusion that I have simply given entirely without context. I deplore this, but a summary must be short, so I did not see how it could be avoided.

Another thing I want to say is that, in the foreword, Jung says that after the publication of *Psychology and Alchemy* he was asked so often "to discuss the relations between the traditional Christ figure and the natural symbols of wholeness" that eventually he decided to do so (p. x).[3] But he says that such an undertaking requires a knowledge and caution that he only possessed in a limited degree. I have already mentioned my own much more limited degree of caution and obviously my deficiencies are enormously greater when it comes to the difference in knowledge. You will, I am well aware, often ask me questions I cannot answer. I can only say that I shall try to admit my ignorance frankly and – if the question is important to the person who asks it or to the class – I will do my best to find out before the next lecture.

The book *Aion*, which was published in 1951, was actually written later than the main outlines of Jung's *opus magnum, Mysterium Coniunctionis*, although the latter was not finished and published until several years after *Aion*. Jung once told me that because *Mysterium Coniunctionis* dealt with the ultimate and most difficult theme of the union of the opposites, although he had the intention of writing it straight through, he constantly found himself obliged to deal with subjects that had to be understood *before* the opposites could be united. One of the most important of these detours is represented by *Aion*. In contradistinction to two other rather long books, which were written in

German in this period ("The Symbolism of the Spirit" and "Formations of the Unconscious") and consisted of rewritten earlier Eranos lectures, *Aion* was entirely new and is perhaps therefore still more of an organic whole than its two immediate predecessors. A part of the fourth and fifth chapters have some material from an Eranos lecture, but this fact has been overestimated in the translator's preface.[4] *Aion* was written before *Answer to Job* and the article "On Synchronicity," which were also entirely new.[5] The "Psychology of the Transference" was originally part of *Mysterium Coniunctionis* and was published by itself before *Aion*.

The name of the book – *Aion* – is the name of a god who represents the creativity of the time principle. This god played a great role in the Mithraic religion and also in late antiquity and in Rome. There are two famous statues of him in the Vatican Museum. Aion could also be called a personification of the whole cosmos as a living whole or – in more modern language – the archetypal personification of the principle of synchronicity.

The book consists of two parts. Jung says in the foreword: "While the contribution of my co-worker, Dr. Marie-Louise von Franz, describes the psychological transition from antiquity to Christianity by analysing the Passion of St. Perpetua, my own investigation seeks, with the help of Christian, Gnostic, and alchemical symbols of the self, to throw light on the change of psychic situation within the 'Christian aeon'" (p. ix).

The two parts are very closely connected, for the second deals with the way in which Christ appears within the assimilation process of a girl's unconscious in those very early times, whereas the first part is mainly concerned with the assimilation of the central symbol of the Self, that is, of the figure of Christ in the matrix of the unconscious throughout the Christian era. It is, therefore, a great pity to separate the two parts from each other, but unfortunately I am obliged to do so on account of time. This matters less, however, because there is an English translation of "Perpetua" in *Spring* (von Franz 1949) where you can all read it and judge it for yourselves.

It is possible that some of you are rather hazy about what is meant by the assimilation of a historical figure or idea in the matrix of the unconscious. To give an example closer to home, I could remind you that the regular students of the Institute some years ago made a collection of the dreams that they had had of Jung and gave it to him. This is a simple example of investigating the way that the matrix of the unconscious, in people interested in the subject, is assimilating or receiving the figure of Jung.

As I mentioned before, *Aion* deals with assimilation of the central symbol of the Self, and I should like to take an example which only comes at the end of the book to give you an idea of why this process is forever going and why it is impossible for it to stay put. This is difficult for us to realize, for our Christian upbringing has been inclined to teach us that the Christian revelation dropped straight from heaven and will remain the same and unchanged forever, amen. Although I renounced this idea decades ago, it constantly reappears as a hidden prejudice, used all too successfully by the animus in his negative aspect.

In the last chapter, "The Structure and Dynamics of the Self," Jung brings two Gnostic and other quaternities to illustrate this theme and finally combines them all in a very interesting but rather complicated formula. He says:

> The formula presents a symbol of the self, for the self is not just a static quantity or constant form, but is also a dynamic process. In the same way, the ancients saw the *imago Dei* in man not as a mere imprint, as a sort of lifeless, stereotyped impression, but as an active force. The four transformations represent a process of restoration or rejuvenation taking place, as it were, inside the self, and comparable to the carbon-nitrogen cycle in the sun, when a carbon nucleus captures four protons (two of which immediately become neutrons) and releases them at the end of the cycle in the form of an alpha particle. The carbon nucleus itself comes out of the reaction unchanged, "like the Phoenix from the ashes." The secret of existence, i.e., the existence of the

> atom and its components, may well consist in a continually repeated process of rejuvenation, and one comes to similar conclusions in trying to account for the numinosity of the archetypes. (par. 411)

When one gets an idea of the movement and change that is apparently taking place all the time in the dynamic process of the Self and remembers that the archetype is anyhow completely beyond our finite comprehension, one gets an idea of how widely different the symbols, by which mankind tries to express the inexpressible, must be in different ages and places. And yet the kernel – like the phoenix and the carbon nucleus – remains essentially the same, so that when one gets a whiff, so to speak, of its essential quality, one can always recognize it as one and the same archetype. *Aion* represents the most helpful opportunity to get this whiff that one can imagine in a book. So many of its innumerable aspects – in the whole Christian era – are given that one can follow the old alchemists' advice to read many books in order to see what they are really all about. Moreover, it is concerned all the way through with the difference between the official Christian symbols and the more empirical, natural symbols of the totality as they appear outside or as they compensate for the Christian dogma. As you know, Jungian psychology regards Christ, like Buddha, as a symbol of the Self, although the Christians often dislike this formulation and would rather regard the Self as a symbol of Christ. Looked at empirically – from a wider standpoint – there is, however, no justification for this latter assumption, although it is natural enough for every religion to regard its symbol as the one revealed truth, they thus narrow their outlook from the start.

But nevertheless Christ is definitely the most important symbol of the Self for us because he is *our* symbol of the Self, with which we grew up – whether our actual education was Christian or not, it is in our blood – and in which the whole of our culture is rooted. We shall discuss this at greater length when we come to the subject in the book, but I should like already here to point out that when Jung realized that before he could finish the *Mysterium Coniunctionis* he must thoroughly understand certain subjects, he was certain to have to go even more deeply than he yet had into the symbol of Christ, for it is absolutely essential in understanding Western civilization.

The book *Aion* gives one a marvelous picture of the way human beings in the past two thousand years have tried to deal with the numinosity of the archetype of the god-man, of which the last worldwide symbol was Christ.

One could perhaps very roughly divide these efforts into attempts to establish a dogma (in an understandable effort to have something fixed and lasting to hold onto in all the dangers and turmoils of life) and attempts to experience the mystery directly. The former only becomes negative when it is used to suppress the latter or when it loses its own meaning. Dogma is always in danger of becoming a "you should" or "it must stay as it is," yet its original content is full of meaning, and Jung makes a great effort to open the eyes of theologians to the fact that the content of their dogma is still effective, still numinous, and that it is only their language and their rigid adherence to outer form that is rendering it so completely impotent today.

This wish to "stay put," to settle certain important points arbitrarily and forever, is to be found already in the early church fathers, and therefore Jung also turns to the Gnostics and alchemists, who were always far more concerned with direct experience. These two tendencies seem to be deeply rooted in the human being for we find them in many places. In the Far East, for instance, Zen Buddhism plays a very similar role to the Gnostics and Alchemists in the West, being wholly concerned with experience and often cutting across the dogma far more ruthlessly than either of its Western counterparts.

It is clear that the tendency toward direct experience will stay closer to the archetype, which seems to be forever renewing itself in the matrix of the unconscious, than any laid down and fixed dogma, so it is very understandable that a lot of *Aion* deals with alchemy and the Gnostics, which represent, as it were, the compensating undercurrent to the surface ruled over by the church and its dogma. The Gnostics were more on the thinking side – they puzzled over and meditated on the mysteries and produced a great deal of profound and original thought. And the alchemists were more on the empirical side, although of course there were individuals who always practiced both. Dorn, for instance, the seventeenth-century alchemist, is also a very profound thinker and puzzles over what he doesn't understand exactly as the Gnostics did, yet he is also very empirical and emphasizes that nothing can be achieved in the alchemical work until you have first achieved it in yourself.

It may surprise some of you that there is so much astrology in *Aion*, particularly if, like myself, you are not personally drawn to astrology, but you must remember that *Aion* was written before Jung's paper on synchronicity, and astrology is essentially based on the principle of synchronicity and could be called a groping towards the becoming conscious of a *quality* in time. To put it much more simply than is legitimate: synchronistic events seem to happen at a time when an archetype approaches consciousness. This gives rise to certain acausally connected images and events that appear or happen either to an individual or to a group of individuals. The archetype itself being outside, or in a different time, is not dependent on either space or time, and the book *Aion* largely deals with how the archetype of the Self – of which the figure of Christ is our chief symbol – was assimilated not only in the matrix of the unconscious but also by consciousness. Time plays a great role in this assimilation, and we see the slow secular change in the archetypal constellation, a slow shifting which is mirrored particularly well as we move along the first and second fish in the astrological sign of Pisces.

We can see by this very clearly that what was absolutely right and suitable in the Middle Ages is no longer so fitting today. It is as if we need to consult the world clock to see where we stand spiritually. In his last article in *Man and His Symbols* (1964), Jung brings a series of dreams dreamt by a twelve-year-old girl. They are full of the most extraordinary archetypal motifs, mainly of death and rebirth. The girl was approaching not only puberty but also the end of her life, for she died a year or two later. Without this knowledge of where she stood spiritually, the dreams would be completely incomprehensible.

When it comes to the process of individuation, all common sense schemata come to an end. On principle, for instance, a girl of twelve is just moving out into life and must be encouraged to do so. But there is nothing of this in her dreams; they are a preparation for death and – if she had been in analysis, which she was not – one would have gotten nowhere by following the general rule for her age. One can only strive to see the quality of the moment in time for that individual, and it is just the same when we consider history.

When you strive to assimilate an archetypal image, you are dealing with something that is partly outside time, so necessarily the past and the future are also present. This is why there is a certain prophetic quality in all methods that exist to deal with the moment in time, in the I-Ching and in astrology, to mention only two examples among many.

As this course is called "The Process of Individuation in *Aion*," you may think as we continue that I mention the process by name very seldom. This is because the whole book is – one could almost say – exclusively concerned with the process of individuation. The assimilation of the figure of Christ, our symbol of the Self – both in the matrix of the unconscious and in consciousness – is individuation *par excellence*, the moving from the conscious, one-sided ego to the total individual. In the first four chapters, Jung explains the process of individuation in his own terminology, as we see it today, and in the following chapters how it was seen by the fathers of the church, by the later church, by the alchemists, and finally by the Gnostics.

As regards the first four chapters, I should just like to tell you that they were not in the book *Aion* as Jung originally wrote it. They were an afterthought, so to speak. After he had written the book, he realized that it would not be comprehensible to people who did not know his psychology, so he added a very clear description of ego, shadow, animus and anima, and the Self. He wrote these – not intellectually – but from the standpoint of feeling and experience. They became, I often think, the clearest and simplest of all his expositions of his psychology, particularly the second and third chapter. They bring a very welcome simplicity, for there is no use denying that – as I said before – the whole book *Aion* is certainly one of the most difficult of all Jung's books to understand.

I

The Ego

I HAVE SUMMARIZED THE FIRST FOUR CHAPTERS particularly briefly, as you are all familiar with the main lines of Jungian psychology. Perhaps this is the most difficult of the four introductory chapters, for we are in the position of Baron Munchausen, who had to pull himself out of the bog by his own plait of hair!

The ego is a complex factor which, though by no means the centre of the total personality, *is* the center of consciousness, for nothing is conscious unless it is related to the ego. Theoretically there is no limit to consciousness; empirically it is exceedingly limited as it stops abruptly when it reaches the unknown, be this in the outer or inner world (par. 1ff).

The ego rests on two apparently different foundations: somatic and psychic, both consisting of conscious and unconscious factors. One can say that the ego stands on the total field of consciousness, on the one hand, and on the sum total of unconscious contents on the other. The latter falls into three groups: 1) that which can be reproduced voluntarily (memory), 2) that which cannot be reproduced voluntarily, and 3) that which has not yet been in consciousness or never will be. The ego, though it "rests" on the total field of consciousness is, of course, *not* identical with it. It is only its point of reference, limited by the somatic factor (par. 8ff).

Although the ego's foundations and environment are relatively unknown, it is a partly conscious factor in itself and is even acquired in the individual's lifetime, apparently from its collision with the somatic factor and the environment and also with inner factors (already in childhood, when we first say "I"), and then it goes on developing from further collisions with the outer and inner world.

Jung has called the total personality the Self, of which the ego is only a part, and just as our limited free will clashes with the facts of the outer world, so it clashes within with the facts of the Self, and just as outside events "happen" to us automatically, so the Self acts on the ego from within as an objective factor, which is much stronger than our free will, however much or little we are willing to admit this fact. Free will is defined by Jung as the libido, which is at the disposition of the ego (par. 9).

Only a limited, formal description of the ego is possible, because any real description would have to take individuality into account, and obviously this is different in every case. The components are indeed everywhere the same, but their combination – their clarity, emotional coloring, and scope – are different in every case. Every ego, as far as one can judge, is individual and even unique, although its stability is relative, because far-reaching alterations in personality sometimes occur. These are by no means always of a pathological nature; on the contrary, they can belong to the highest development and thus be wholly normal (par. 9).

The ego – as point of reference – has a very significant part to play, and it is not surprising that the prejudice of it being the center of the personality flourished for so long and still persists so obstinately. But once the existence of a psyche outside consciousness is realized by experience, the absolute position of the ego becomes relative. It is impossible to say how large or how small the influence of the ego is, but it is certainly unwise to underestimate its dependence on the unconscious (par. 10).

We saw that the unconscious from the standpoint of conscious psychology falls into three groups, but, from the standpoint of the psychology of personality, there is a twofold division, in brief the personal unconscious and the collective unconscious. The former belongs to the individual personality and could just as well be conscious, whereas the latter is, as it were, the same everywhere and in everyone. Of course, this is only a hypothesis, yet it is forced upon us by the nature of the empirical material exactly as instinct, which manifests in an individual, is a piece of a quite general instinctive foundation (par. 11).

II

The Shadow

THIS REPRESENTS ONE OF THE CLEAREST DESCRIPTIONS of the shadow in Jung's writings, though it is very short.

Except in the rather rare cases where people are living below themselves, the shadow is a moral problem *par excellence*, that challenges the whole ego personality (par. 14). (I have been here for over thirty years and have naturally seen many come and go, and without exception only those who were willing and able to face their shadow went on into further development.) Realizing it means painstaking and painful working, but it is relatively simple as the personal shadow is mainly in the personal unconscious. The real difficulty is the emotion attached. Emotion is *not* an activity of the individual but something that happens to him where his adaptation is weakest and causes obsession or even possession! Here – however differentiated and civilized we may be in consciousness – we all behave like primitives who are the passive victims of their affects and singularly incapable of moral judgment. We behave in just the same way where our adaptation is weakest (par. 15).

Although a good deal of the shadow is easily – if painfully – assimilated, the parts that are projected are often incredibly obstinate. Getting back these projections, Jung says, is a moral achievement that goes far beyond the ordinary.

Projections isolate us by surrounding us with a veil of delusion that obscures reality entirely. As an example, a patient age forty-five once said: "I can never admit I have wasted the best twenty-five years of my life." It is a tragedy to see people bring their own lives and other people's to disaster without being able to see how the whole tragedy originates in themselves. They bewail a faithless world and spin a cocoon that – if they cannot or will not cut through it – will in the end completely envelop them. This explains why, in many older people, one can get no contact whatever (par. 18).

A great difficulty in realizing the shadow lies in its being contaminated by the animus or anima. The shadow is always of the same sex, so as soon as there are signs of the other sex in us we can suspect the presence of anima or animus. These are far more autonomous and beyond our reach than the personal shadow. But behind the personal shadow is also the archetype of the shadow and, comparatively easy as it is to recognize the relative evil of our own shadow, it is always a shattering experience to glimpse the face of absolute evil (par. 19).

I would like to comment on this last point. One can understand and even accept jealousy, prestige, egoistic motives, and so on, both in oneself and other people, but sometimes – mainly when there is a psychosis – one really looks in the face of absolute evil and then it is absolutely shattering. There are people who have no moral brakes as to murder, for instance, and with a completely possessed face will tell you that they pray for so-and-so's (or perhaps one's own) death. Then it is shattering because the human being is no longer there and you are confronted with the devil himself. One has only to remember the gas chambers of the concentration camps and there you see the face of absolute evil, unveiled and unashamed.

III

The Syzygy: Animus and Anima

ALTHOUGH A GOOD DEAL LONGER, this chapter again contains one of the clearest descriptions of the animus and anima that Jung has ever given. The beginning deals with the mother complex and is so important that I translated it as soon as it came out in German and lent it to all the devouring mothers and eaten sons who worked with me. As a woman, I put it this way, but Jung makes it very clear that the guilt is very evenly divided between the two. The mother is far too anxious to keep the son wrapped up in cotton wool and the son is always lamed by the remembrance of all she can do for him; therefore he cannot stick to his efforts to conquer the resistant world but always falls back on the hope that everything he wants will be given to him, as in his earliest days, by the mother. Neither of them want such an unsatisfactory state of affairs but all too often they are both – entirely unknown to themselves – caught in the fascination of the *hieros gamos*, the old sacred image of the marriage of mother and son (par.20ff).

The projection of the anima onto the mother can only be dissolved from the man's side when he can realize that the image in his psyche is not identical with the mother but also includes the sister, the beloved woman, the daughter, and, beyond these mortal figures, the heavenly goddess and the chthonic Baubo. This anima figure represents for him the loyalty which life often forbids him to keep with one woman – above all with the mother – and, though the anima entangles him in life's most terrible paradoxes, it is yet the factor – just because she is so dangerous – that can draw out everything that is in him. She demands his greatest from a man, and if he has it in him, she will also succeed in producing it (par. 24).

Jung says that he purposely uses dramatic and mythological language in speaking of the anima, for she does not lend herself to rational scientific language. We often try to reason her away, it is true, but only to find – or at least to make it very obvious to our environment – that we have fallen into her hands and that she has possessed us from behind, just while we were proving so conclusively that she is a mere theoretic formulation (par. 25)!

The anima is no invention of consciousness but is a spontaneous product of the unconscious, of terrifying autonomy, and is balanced in the psychology of women by the figure of the animus. Just as the mother is the first carrier of this archetype in men, so the father in women. The animus corresponds to the paternal logos, just as the anima corresponds to the maternal eros. Just as eros is less developed in men than logos, so logos often seems no more than a regrettable mistake in women whose true nature is relationship. It is full of opinions instead of reflections and gives rise to endless misunderstandings in the environment. The animus is very partial to argument, and he can drive an originally clear-thinking man to such despair that he can even become the animus of his own anima and argue just like a woman himself. Not that the animus is the only sinner in this respect; the man can be quite equally annoying with his moods and the personal vanity and touchiness of his anima. The animus calls out the anima and vice versa, whether they fall in love with each other (a special case of love at first sight) or indulge in endless and fruitless arguments (par. 26ff).

In both positive and negative aspects, there is always a lot of animosity in a relation which is predominately an anima-animus relation, and very often it runs its own course and the human beings do not know afterwards what happened to them. Consciousness has been held captive by the powerfully suggestive effect of the archetype (par. 34).

It is – as mentioned before – much easier to gain insight into the shadow than into the animus and anima. Our whole upbringing has taught us that we are not one hundred percent pure gold but there is no such moral education as regards the animus and anima, and we are so used to men having irrational moods and women fixed, irrational opinions that we even doubt if we are not meddling too much in nature itself by awaking things that would be better left asleep, when we try to become conscious of them (par. 35).

When we are convinced that the projections caused by animus and anima are better dissolved, so that we may at last see reality as it is, we are treading a new path, and the moral and intellectual exertion that is required to dissolve these projections is terrific. The childish prejudice that "we know what we think" has to be entirely overcome, and we have to move into an entirely new world of psychological experience (par. 39).

The autonomy of the collective unconscious expresses itself above all through the figures of the animus and anima. If there is sufficient harmony between conscious and unconscious, they are like functions between the two, but tension between conscious and unconscious immediately personifies them and they behave as autonomous figures or even demons. And we must never forget that though their effects and contents can be made conscious, they themselves remain factors transcending consciousness, archetypes that can never be integrated or subdued by the human will. They always remain autonomous factors which must forever be reckoned with. We can never deal with the unconscious and settle it once for all; indeed if we could, we would become one-sided monsters. We can, however, learn to live with the animus and anima and encourage them to compensate the narrowness of consciousness, but we can never eliminate them (par. 40).

They are indeed, as Jung says, quite literally the father and mother of all the dramatic and even disastrous entanglements of fate and have long been recognized as such, as a divine pair, the one – in accordance with his logos nature – characterized by the pneuma, Nous and Hermes, and the other – in accordance with her eros nature – characterized as Aphrodite, Selene, Persephone, and Hecate. The ancients – realizing their true nature quite rightly – called them gods, and the more we realize this the better, for their power increases to the degree that it remains unconscious, just as typhoid can spread widest when its source is undiscovered. Although the ancient Greeks saw them more plastically, the animus and anima are not missing in Christianity; in fact they occupy the highest place as Christ and his bride, the church. Such parallels help us to realize the immense influence wielded by these two figures that complement our conscious life (par. 41).

The shadow *must* be realized before we can see the animus and anima. And as the shadow needs the relation to a partner before we can realize it, so the animus and anima require a relation to someone of the opposite sex, because only in such a relation do we see or suffer from their effects. This gives rise to a triad, and the missing fourth in man is the wise old man and in woman the chthonic mother, which leads us to the next chapter on the Self (par.42).

IV

The Self

THE INCREASE OF SELF-KNOWLEDGE ACQUIRED by investigation of the shadow and the animus and anima, and above all the withdrawal of projections, leads to a considerable change in the ego personality.

This is indeed a never ending process and can be positive or negative in effect. This depends mainly on the attitude of the ego, which needs, on the one hand, to be firmly rooted in the field of consciousness and, on the other, to be capable of discriminating the autonomous figures of the unconscious and to allow for their constant effect on consciousness. If either of these *conditiones sine qua non* are missing, it can easily lead to a psychic catastrophe: either the ego is assimilated by the Self or vice versa, either of which leads to a dangerous, even disastrous, inflation (par. 44).

Certain virtues, such as attentiveness, conscientiousness, patience, and so on, are indispensable here on the moral side, as well as an accurate observation of the unconscious and objective self-criticism on the intellectual side. It is a constant navigation between Scylla and Charybdis: we cannot afford to sacrifice the conscious entirely to the unconscious or vice versa but must forever hold the balance between the two as well as we can (par. 46).

This will lead inevitably to the dreaded conflicts of duty. Real morality begins where the penal code stops. This higher authority can be called the "will of God" or, as the Oxford Dictionary describes an act of God, as the "action of uncontrollable natural forces." The latter fits modern rationalism better, but the former is more in accord with the habitus of our ancestral psychic life (par. 48ff).

Psychology is the only science that we cannot pursue with the intellect alone, for it is impossible to grasp it in its totality intellectually, for the intellect – that god of modern consciousness – is a great cheat and deceiver outside its own field. It knows nothing of feeling values, for instance, and the latter are of paramount importance in psychology. Intellect and feeling are hard to drive in double harness. Directly we try to do this, a man comes up against his anima, and a woman against her animus, but coming to grips with this problem is the *conditio sine qua non* of opening the way to the higher union, the *coniunctio oppositorum* and to the Self. There is no escaping coming to grips with this problem, it is the indispensable prerequisite for wholeness (par. 53ff).

Wholeness – even with its mandala symbols – may at first sight seem to be a mere abstract idea, but it is something that exists and can be experienced. In fact, it must be experienced or one has no idea what it is. We may read up all the clinical symptoms of a bad illness, for instance, but only the man who has had it really knows what it is (par. 59).

Psychic facts cannot be described, they can only be known by experience, and fear of the unconscious is such a much more general condition than we realize that there will always be critics who prefer to deny its existence. "There ain't no such bird" (the duck-billed platypus) and the moons of Jupiter in the time of Galileo were also denied in face of the actual visible facts (par. 61).

Outside psychology the figures of the shadow, the animus and anima, and the Self will meet with most understanding from people who have some knowledge of comparative mythology. They will recognize the figures of the shadow, the syzygy pair, and finally the Self as the *eidos* (basic pattern) behind the supreme ideas of unity and totality (par. 63).

These parallels are important, for so-called metaphysical concepts have lost connection with their roots in natural experience, and we need to see them again in their true and original meaning. What these so-called metaphysical ideas mean is a genuine problem today. "How has the death of Christ brought us redemption when no one feels redeemed?" and so on, with the idea of Jesus as a God-man, the doctrine of the Trinity, the Last Supper and so on. The vast majority of people have no idea how such ideas can be connected with the material world they live in (par. 65).

Up until say 1933, mythological ideas also hardly existed and were thought completely crazy. But then a myth (Wotan) broke over Europe, and since then we see on all sides that the world of myths is as vital as ever and has been entirely unaffected by centuries of reason and enlightenment. This end result is a true *antimimon pneuma*, a false spirit of arrogance, hysterics, woolly-mindedness, criminal amorality, and doctrinaire stupidity, a creator of cheap spiritual goods, spurious art, philosophical stammering, and Utopian swindle, fit only to be fed wholesale to the mass man of today. "That," Jung ends this chapter by saying, "is what the post-Christian spirit looks like" (par. 67).

V

Christ, a Symbol of the Self

WE COME NOW TO THE ESSENTIAL THEME OF THE BOOK.

The Luciferian days in which we live have often – from many sides – been compared with the eschatological events foretold in the New Testament. The coming of Christ's opposite – the Antichrist – and his usurpation of the power is clearly foretold in the Apocalypse, showing that the *anima Christiana* in those very early days knew quite well that an enantiodromia was certain and inevitable (par. 68).

Christ is the still-living cultural myth of our age. He is the hero of our culture – in our blood, however we were brought up. He is the center of our mandala, and – whether we know it or not – he is in us and we are in him. His kingdom of heaven is our symbol of the treasure hard to attain and the pearl of great price: the Self (par. 69).

In our age Christ still represents the archetype of the Self. He represents a divine totality, unspoiled by sin. We find descriptions of Christ as exactly this in the writings of most of the old fathers of the church whom Jung quotes at considerable length: Tertullian, St. Augustine, and so on. Jung says: "There can be no doubt that the original Christian conception of the *imago Dei* embodied in Christ meant all-embracing totality that even includes the animal side of man. But nevertheless the Christ symbol lacks wholeness in the modern psychological sense for it does not include the dark side but splits this off as Lucifer, Christ's opponent from the beginning (par. 74).

This was fully realized but was watered down very early by the doctrine of the *privatio boni*, first started by Origen (185–254 A.D.). Evil was deprived of its substance by the idea that it was a mere accidental absence of good and the stage was set for the disastrous idea that "all good belongs to God and all evil to man" (Tatian, second century A.D.) (par. 74).

It must be emphasized, however, that it was the church fathers who tried to guarantee a light wholeness to Christ by the doctrine of the *privatio boni*. The Gnostics tackled the problem of evil on a much broader basis than the orthodox Church. They were much nearer the psychological truth that good and evil are two equal opposites, such as light and darkness and heat and cold. Irenaeus, for instance, records the Gnostic teaching that Christ cut off his shadow from himself, an idea that leads directly to the Antichrist and all we are suffering at his hands today. The Antichrist developed in legend as a perverse imitator, a spirit of evil that follows in Christ's footsteps as the shadow follows the body (par. 75).

If we see Christ then as a psychic manifestation of the Self, the Antichrist would correspond to the shadow of the Self. In the empirical Self of psychology, light and shadow form a paradoxical unity, but in the orthodox Christian concept the archetype is split into two irreconcilable halves, leading ultimately to just that duality which the church fathers were trying to avoid, for the doctrine of the *privatio boni* was largely thought up as an answer to the Manichean heresy (par. 76).

The dogmatic figure of Christ is so sublime and spotless that everything inevitably turns dark beside it, a fact which was realized fully by the writer of the Apocalypse. The coming of Antichrist is not just a prophetic prediction, it is based on the inexorable psychological law that anything too light will be followed by an enantiodromia into its opposite (par. 77).

Again and again, however, this psychological law was overlooked and forgotten. The weakness in the Christian disposition is that it ever and again strives for the spiritual heights without remembering or realizing that such a one-sided endeavor is always doomed to clash with man's earthbound passion to conquer matter and master the earth. Yet it could have been remembered, for Christ clashed with Satan right at the beginning of his career, and we hear of "a reign of a thousand years" and of "the coming of the Antichrist" as if two royal brothers had divided the worlds between them, Christ taking the kingdom of the spirit and the Antichrist (or Satan) the kingdom of this world (par. 78).

Just as we have to remember the gods of antiquity to recognize the psychological value of the animus and anima, so Christ is our nearest analogy of the Self and its meaning. Christ's attributes undoubtedly mark him out as a manifestation of the Self but – from the psychological angle – he is only one half of the archetype, the other half appearing as the Antichrist. Both are Christian symbols and have the same meaning as Christ – being crucified between the two thieves. This inevitably involves us in a crucifixion of the ego between these two irreconcilable opposites. Of course, there can be no final extinction of the ego, for that would destroy all possibility of consciousness. The ego has to submit, however, to a continual crucifixion between the opposites, to those dreaded conflicts in duty, which were mentioned before (par. 79).

Jung goes on to say that the splitting off of the shadow was increased by the doctrine of the *summum bonum* and the related *privatio boni* and quotes many of the old church fathers on the subject. I will only mention one typical example of these, where Basil (fourth century A.D.) asserts that evil has no substance of its own and is only a "mutilation of the soul." But who mutilated the soul? Jung says "the basic flaw in Basil's argument is the *petitio principii* [assuming from the beginning what you want to prove at the end] that lands him in insoluble contradictions: it is laid down from the start that the independent existence of evil must be denied even in face of the eternity of the devil as asserted by dogma" (par. 85).

This is really the basic flaw that one can see in all the many quotations here from such church fathers as Irenaeus, St. Augustine, John Chrysostom and Dionysius the Aeropagite. Even the much later Thomas Aquinas (thirteenth century) asserts: "Evil is not a being, whereas good is a being" (par. 91) and that a "thing is the whiter, the less it is mixed with black" (ibid.). He does not draw the obvious conclusion, however, that a "thing is the blacker, the less it is mixed with white."

I will leave you to study all these many interesting quotations for yourselves and end this part (for this chapter falls into two halves) with Jung's conclusion that we might just as well say that the arctic winter is only an absence of heat, it would not prevent our bodies from getting frostbite of the severest kind. Did God create only the heat? We can agree with St. Augustine when he says, "All natures are good," but are they really good enough to prevent their badness being equally obvious (par. 95)?

It would be sheer mockery to speak of things that have happened – like the concentration camps – as mere "accidental lack of perfection" (par. 96). But psychology does not pretend to know what good and evil are in *themselves*. They are a more or less subjective judgment: good is what seems suitable, acceptable, or valuable from a certain point of view, and evil is its opposite. There certainly are things which are dangerous and even extremely evil, and it is most unsafe to gloss over this fact for it only gives us a false sense of security which is nothing but unconsciousness (par. 97).

Today – with the world in the state it is – it is more important than ever to see the evil that lurks within us all. Psychology is an empirical science and deals with realities, and Jung's criticism of the *privatio boni* holds only inasfar as psychological experience goes. From the scientific point of view – as must be obvious to everybody – it is founded on a *petitio principii* and what comes out at the end is what you put in at the beginning. But its very existence proves a human tendency to give the priority to good, to increase the good by every foul or fair means in its power and to diminish the bad. From this point of view, the *privatio boni* may therefore be a psychological truth. But in our own field of experience good and bad always turn out to be equal opposites, and one always leads to one other (par. 98).

This fact was correctly appreciated in the so-called Clementine Homilies (second century). The unknown author understands good and evil as the right and left hands of God and views the whole of creation as a pair of opposites. The whole of what Jung says about these Clementine Homilies is very interesting but – as it gets more complicated – I will not try to sum it up further here.

Jung says at the end that this unknown author is closely related to the early Jewish Christian Church where – according to Epiphanius – we find the Ebionite idea that God had two sons, the elder Satan and the younger Christ (par. 103).

After quoting more material from the Ascension of Isaiah, Jung goes on to say that we might risk the conjecture that the problem of the Yahwistic God image – constellated by the Book of Job – continued to be discussed in Gnostic circles and in syncretistic Judaism, and that the Christian answer – decision in favor of God being all good – did not satisfy the conservative Jews. Inside Christianity the doctrine of the two antithetical sons of God spread to the Bogomils and the Catharists, and in Judaism it found a lasting expression in the two sides of the cabalistic Tree of the Sephiroth (par. 94f).

Jung goes on to give a number of passages from Hebrew literature which were collected for him by a rabbinical scholar, Zwi Werblowsky, who has since lectured more than once at the Institute. I will not go into the detail of these quotations (some of you know this literature infinitely better than I do) and will only venture the general remark that God himself seems to have a hard time in making his mercy repress his wrath (par. 106).

The Cabala evidently had an influence on Jacob Boehme, for we find exactly the same ambivalence in his writings between the love of God and his "wrath fire" (par. 111).

I have often quoted in courses what Jung says at the beginning of *Psychology and Religion* when defining the standpoint of his psychology. He says:

> This standpoint is exclusively phenomenological, that is, it is concerned with occurrences, events, experiences – in a word, with facts. Its truth is a fact and not a judgment. When psychology speaks, for instance, of the motif of the virgin birth, it is only concerned with the fact that there is such an idea, but it is not concerned with the question of whether such an idea is true or false in any other sense. The idea is psychologically true inasmuch as it exists. Psychological existence is subjective in so far as an idea occurs in only one individual. But it is objective in so far as that idea is shared by a society – by a *consensus gentium*. (1938, par. 4)

As psychology is not metaphysics, one cannot use its statements concerning equivalent opposites to establish a metaphysical dualism nor can such an opinion be imputed to psychology. There could be no discrimination or cognition without equivalent opposites. But we cannot assume that these opposites are at the same time *eo ipso* a quality of the observed object. It is more likely to be our own consciousness that names or perhaps even creates these differences (par. 112). I mention here – though it is not in the book – the fact that we often dream of things which are just coming over the border of consciousness as *double*. Later, when they are fully in consciousness, they turn out to be one. I think – though I may be wrong – that Jung means something of this kind here when he points out that we can only discriminate by means of the opposite, yet we cannot assume *for certain* that they are a quality of an object that is anyhow beyond our comprehension. This really explains why psychology can *never* pass judgment on metaphysical statements, except to say that they cannot be proved.

Jung goes on to say that he has gone into the doctrine of the *privatio boni* at such length because it is largely responsible for too much optimism concerning evil in human nature. Yet early Christianity, with unerring logic, balanced Christ with an Antichrist (par. 113).

Moreover – as early as Basil – we meet with a tendency to attribute evil to the disposition of the human soul and yet at the same time to give it a "nonexistent" character. Moreover, according to Basil, evil originates in human frivolity and owes its very existence to mere negligence. Evil thus becomes a *quantité négligeable* and the human psyche becomes its birthplace. The church fathers can hardly have realized what a fatal power they were ascribing to the soul, a negative inflation, that is, a demonic claim to power on the part of the unconscious. Yet this unavoidable consequence was anticipated in the figure of the Antichrist and is now reflected in the course of contemporary events, as the Christian eon of the fishes is reaching its end (par. 114).

But in the world of Christian ideas, Christ undoubtedly represents the Self. Jung says in a footnote that it has been objected that Christ cannot have been a valid symbol of the Self but rather only an illusory substitute. Jung disagrees with this objection, particularly as regards the past, the prepsychological age. At that time, Christ did not merely symbolize wholeness, he *was* wholeness. The idea of totality, at any given time, is just as total as one is oneself. Now that psychological criticism has become possible, a greater degree of wholeness has opened up. But who can guarantee that our conception of totality is not as much in need of completion in its turn as the degree represented in the figure of Christ (par. 115n)?

In the text, Jung goes on to show that the figure of Christ has the main attributes of wholeness:

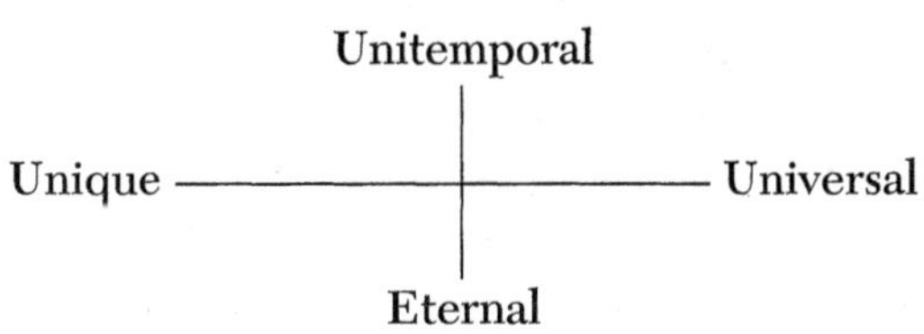

As man, Christ is unitemporal and unique; as God, universal and eternal. But if theology describes Christ as only good and spiritual, it is necessary to include the Antichrist in the following diagram:

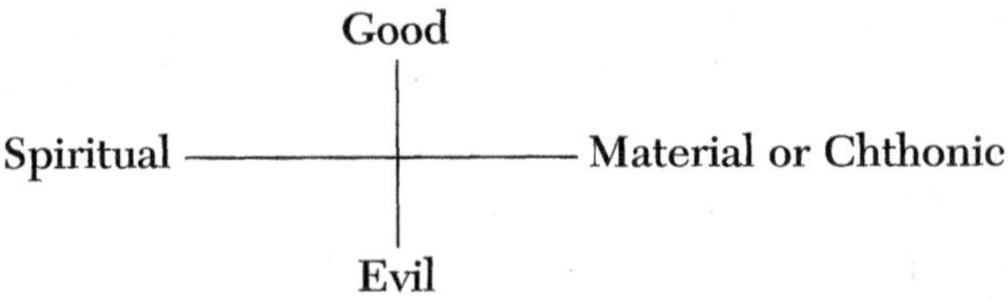

Therefore, in this age, we need no longer separate the two but can see them both in the Self. This is no new idea, for according to Hippolytus, it was already known to the Naassene Gnostics, to say nothing of the alchemists. It is an essential part of the process of individuation (par. 117).

Jung goes on to point out that Christ was early known as the *principium individuationis* and goes on to prove this in the rather complicated teaching of Basilides, concerning the threefold sonship. He compares this threefold sonship with Christ's three natures and with spirit, soul, and body. As mortal man, Christ separated these three natures, and as son of Mary, Christ brought down consciousness into the third formless and material sonship – the body – and was thus the prototype of the principle of individuation (par. 118ff).

In his conclusion to this chapter Jung sums up what he has been saying – at the risk of repeating himself – because of the enormous importance of the material.

He emphasizes that the parallel that he has drawn between Christ and the Self is not to be taken as anything more than psychological, just as the fish parallel is mythological. There is no question of an intrusion into metaphysics, that is, faith. The ancients felt that they had illuminated the image of Christ with the symbol of the fish, just as the alchemists felt about the stone. Both symbols disappeared in the course of time. But the statements of alchemists attach such importance to their symbol of the stone, one wonders whether they did not regard Christ as a symbol of the lapis, rather than the other way around? Modern psychology is faced with the same question: is the Self a symbol of Christ or vice versa (par. 121ff)?

Jung's experience has led him to the latter alternative, for we find the living archetype of the Self everywhere. Jung emphasizes that he tries to consider the material objectively, as an art historian, for instance, would. He is *not* concerned with confessions of faith but with evident scientific facts (par. 123).

When one takes the archetype of the Self as the active agent – and thus Christ as a symbol of the Self – one must bear in mind the difference between perfection and completeness. Christ is the ideal of perfection, whereas the Self is far from perfect but denotes completion and is therefore a paradox. Where this archetype predominates, completeness is forced upon us, against all our conscious strivings. St. Paul realized this when he said: "I find then a law, that, when I would do good, evil is present with me" (Rom. 7:21).

The Christian image also corresponds to this situation: Christ is the perfect man who is crucified. Whenever the archetype of the Self is constellated, we are crucified like Christ. Redemption does not mean that we escape our burden, and only a man who is approaching completeness knows how unbearable man is to himself. Jung says that he does not see that any valid objection could be raised from the Christian standpoint against our accepting the task of individuation, imposed on us by Nature herself. If we do so voluntarily and consciously, we are at least spared its happening to us against our will in a negative form, just as, if we have to descend into a deep pit, we had better set about it with a ladder and all the necessary precautions than to fall backward into it (par. 124ff).

During the war, Jung used to say very convincingly that what had really happened to Germany was that the process of individuation was not recognized by any individuals and had therefore gone into the whole nation and become a collective thing and thus simply happened unconsciously and, as with all things belonging to the archetype and individuation, if they are not realized they take place disastrously instead of meaningfully. I have brought Germany in as an example of repressed individuation, but really you see it much more clearly in individuals.

I may remind you again of those two childhood dreams of mine where I had the choice of walking out into the opposites or of being hung between them by Fate – that puts it in a very graphic and simple form.

The irreconcilable nature of the opposites in Christian psychology is due to their moral exaggeration. (They have got infinitely worse. In their primitive form, the opposites were not really so bad but they have now reached such a point that they have become irreconcilable.) This exaggeration seems natural to us, although, looked at historically, it is a legacy from the Old Testament with its emphasis on righteousness in the eyes of the law. Such an influence is notably lacking in the East, in the philosophical religions of India and China. (In Tao there is not such a terrible split between good and evil as that under which we suffer.) Without stopping to discuss the question of whether this exacerbation of the opposites, much as it increases suffering, may not after all correspond to a higher degree of truth, I should merely like to express the hope that the present world situation may be looked upon in the light of the psychological rule alluded to above. Today humanity, as never before, is split into two apparently irreconcilable halves. The psychological rule says that when an inner situation is not made conscious, it happens outside, as fate. That is to say, when the individual remains undivided and does not become conscious of his inner contradictions, the world must perforce act out the conflict and be torn into opposite halves (par. 121ff).

Jung wrote a paper called "Present and Future" (1957), in which he says that the only thing one can possibly do in this present situation is to look at one's own shadow and begin to heal the split, at any rate in one place, for then one is really doing something for the situation. At a meeting of the Psychological Club of Zürich, Jung was once asked whether he thought that the atom bomb would be used, and he replied that it depended on the number of individuals who could stand the clash of the opposites in themselves. If enough could, he thought that we would somehow, though not in any dramatic way, just slide around the final catastrophe, but if there were not enough people to do this, then he was afraid that our civilization would simply vanish as many have done in the past, though now it would be much worse. This made a terrific impression on me which was very much rubbed in by a woman who came from Germany. She had held a very high position during the war in Germany and always wanted America or England or the German government to use a magic wand. When talking to me about the situation, I told her the above. At that moment we were just getting into my car, and she managed to put her hand so that her fingers were crushed quite badly in the mechanism of the seat – though in the seventeen years I drove the car and in the years when Marie-Louise von Franz has driven it, nobody else has ever managed to get themselves even scratched in such a way. I told Jung about it, and he said: "Yes, exactly, she would not believe it, she did not mean to see it." She had been in analysis before the war and had gone back to Germany and had got caught by the idea that anything could be done by an act of Parliament. That is a little example of the thing working from the outside if you won't accept it within, which is the only place where we can do anything, and the fact that this is possible does give a meaning to every life. Even if we can only give a grain, that grain is of value.

I have been asked by Dr. Sanford to define what was meant by the term "the Passion," because he had never seen it written or expressly stated. I am merely going to say what I think it means and am not making a theological statement. As I understand it, the Passion refers to Christ's sufferings in the Garden of Gethsemane and at the crucifixion – the absolute torture which Christ went through at the end of his life. One could say that before the Passion he had separated from the devil "for a season" – as at the time of the temptation – and had always taught the doctrine of a purely loving God. It might be said that when he prayed: "O my Father, if it be possible, let this cup pass from me; nevertheless not as I will, but as thou wilt," that then he realized for the first time that God was not only a loving Father, for if so, would he crucify his only son? Can a God who is only loving abandon a man who had done his best, as Christ had, to such hellish torture as death upon the cross? As I see it, he then realized and had to suffer from the opposites in God, and he did so consciously and thus is, particularly at his crucifixion, the symbol of individuation, of accepting both opposites. If he had refused that agony and run away, and there were plenty of people who liked him well enough to hide him, he might then have gone into an agonizing old age where terrible things might have happened to him from the outside, but because he accepted it, he became the symbol of a process of individuation which was lived to the end. I have never seen anybody who could have become conscious of the conflict within themselves and has run away from it who has not had a far worse fate coming to them from the outside, though they themselves thought they were the victims of impossible circumstances.

The question comes up: When Jung talks of the crucifixion as a symbol of individuation, I wonder whether in the crucifixion where Christ's human body is crucified, whether it is the sacrifice of the body to attain individuation? This is pure speculation, but I wonder whether actually, in a very real sense, individuation does not mean sacrificing the body, the death of the body?

This may be right; whether one really does individuate before death is open to doubt, but there is certainly a prestage of individuation in which the body is very much still there. Take, for example, Jeanne Féry, a case of possession in the sixteenth century. The girl was completely possessed by devils, and then a figure came up in her which the devils called Mary Magdalene, and slowly that figure replaced the demons and also forced the archbishop to take the girl out of the convent and have her in his house, which led to the most malevolent scandal when his whole diocese went up in the air – yet he had to do it. Or there is the case of the Prophet Hosea who had to marry the prostitute. God set him a question: "What are you going to do about it?" No doubt he fell in love with her, but he had to answer God's question in his body, and that I call, at any rate, a prestage to individuation. Again, think of *Answer to Job:* God did not know the answer and tortured Job to get it. Certainly, at any rate, the before stages of the process of individuation very much include the body. Kallikrates said that you could not repent of those sins which you have not committed – a very wise saying, Jung says, for those who understand it, and a brilliant opportunity for those who misunderstand it.

The great accentuation of opposites in our Christian psychology is due to the strong accent on morality, which is a legacy from the Old Testament. Such an influence is notably lacking in the East, in India and China, for instance. Jung expresses the hope that we may learn to look at our own world situation in light of the psychological rule of the opposites, for today humanity is split – as never before – into two apparently irreconcilable halves. It is a psychological rule that if an inner situation is not made conscious, it will happen outside. That is, if the individual does not become conscious of his own inner contradictions, the world will be forced to act out the conflict and be torn into opposite halves (par. 126).

VI

The Sign of the Fishes

First I would like to remind you of the curious synchronistic fish events that happened to Jung while he was writing this part of *Aion*. They are described in his paper "Synchronicity: An Acausal Connecting Principle" (Jung 1952b, par. 826ff).

We come now to the theme of the fishes, which occupies nearly half the book.

I would like just to comment here that the fish is the symbol par excellence for what takes us down into the unconscious, and of all symbols of Christ it is perhaps the most meaningful in this respect. Moreover, our whole era has taken place in the sign of the fishes; the age of Aquarius is only now on the threshold, so to speak. There is always a disturbing time at the end of an era, when moving from one astrological sign into another. Jung worked out that we do not move into the fishes until the third millenium, but the first stars of Aquarius are already affecting us now.

Jung begins by saying that the figure of Christ is not as simple as one could wish, not only because of the great difference between the figure in the Synoptic gospels compared with the account in St. John, but because – right from the days of primitive Christianity – he shares a great many symbols with the devil.

To mention only a few: the lion, snake, bird, raven, eagle, and, of course, the fish. Apart from the snake, the fish is one of the oldest symbols (par. 127).

The fish symbol in Christianity has a long prehistory, such as the Babylonian fish-god Oannes and the Phoenician goddess Derceto-Atargatis. We find it also in India as the redeemer fish Manu (par. 127).

As it is such a widespread symbol, we need not be surprised at it turning up at any time and in any place. But its sudden activation and early identification with Christ leads one to suspect a further reason, which we find in astrology and indeed – as is well known – Christ was born as the spring point passed from Ares (the ram) to Pisces (the fish) (par. 128).

Jung goes into a good deal of astrology here, which I will leave you to read for yourselves, only mentioning that the *coniunctio* between Jupiter (a beneficent star) and Saturn (a maleficent one) comes up again and again, and that this *coniunctio* has the meaning of a union of extreme opposites. In the year 7 B.C., for instance, this famous *coniunctio* took place three times in the sign of the fishes. This *coniunctio* was further qualified by the fact that Mars was in opposition to it, which is peculiarly characteristic of Christianity, because Mars is the planet correlated with the instincts. Jung says that if we accept Gerhardt's calculations, the sun was in the Twins when Christ was born, which reminds one at once of the theme of the hostile brothers, especially in Egypt (par. 128ff).

The astrological predictions that were probably already known in antiquity all point to this double aspect, and one therefore understands how suitable the myth of Christ and the Antichrist must have seemed to contemporary astrological intellects (par. 133).

The Talmud (certainly before the sixth century) also bears witness to the antithetical nature of the fishes and speaks of the wars of the tanninim (sea monsters), the wars of Gog and Magog. An eleventh-century Talmud commentator, Solomon Jezchaki, remarks that the tanninim are fishes, which is important because it takes the battle of the fishes as an eschatological event (like the fight between Behemoth and Leviathan) and because it is probably the earliest testimony of the antithetical nature of the fishes (par. 133).

There are a great many astrological predictions given with most complicated numbers, which I omit because I admit they are beyond me, and I take up the line again with Joachim of Flora (twelfth century) who announced a new era of the Holy Ghost. He dated the secret inception of this new era (even to become a new status of the world) with the founding of the Benedictine Order (around 534) which brings us close to the year 530, which the Talmud prophesied would be critical. Joachim's age itself was noted for its spiritual instability and the many wild new sects that sprang up, but monasticism – so near to Joachim's heart that he saw it as the true vehicle of the era of the Holy Ghost – was injected with new life by the founding of the mendicant orders. Apart from this, there was a widespread religious inflation, the well-known dangerous result of identifying with the Divine, in this case with the Holy Ghost. The numinosity was heightened by the temporal synchronicity of the age in which Joachim lived, the beginning of the sphere of the anti-Christian fish. Although Joachim himself did not go nearly as far as many of the sects that began at this time, he was nevertheless condemned by the Church, as most people have been who were gripped by an archetype. And in Joachim's case it is very understandable, for his attitude toward the Christian Church came very near to open insurrection (par. 137ff).

Jung points out that as the eon of the fishes has been ruled by the archetypal motif of the hostile brothers, the approach of the next Platonic month, Aquarius, will constellate the problem of the union of opposites, and only the individual can solve this problem in his own process of individuation. The declaration of the *Assumptio Mariae* is an example of the way symbols develop through the ages and, as is well known, this came about from below from the visions of the masses at bottom, from the urge of the archetype to realize itself (par. 142).

The repercussions of the movement of the Holy Ghost led to four minds that had an immense influence on the future: Albertus Magnus, Thomas Aquinas, Roger Bacon, and Meister Eckhart. Some people have also rightly seen the Holy Ghost movement as the forerunner of the Reformation. And synchronistically, Latin alchemy also began around the twelfth and thirteenth centuries. The *lapis* of alchemy is a parallel to the "new rock" with which the Holy Ghost was also compared (par. 143f).

Jung then returns, after many parallels with the *lapis,* to Christ as the fish. According to Doelger, who investigated the fish symbol very thoroughly, the Christian fish symbol first appeared in Alexandria about 200 A.D. and the baptismal bath was also described as a *piscina* (fishpond) very early. This presupposes that the believers were fish and is indeed already suggested in the gospels where some of the disciples were fishermen whom Christ wanted to make "fishers of men" (Matt. 4:19). Christ himself uses the miraculous draught of fishes as a prototype of Peter's missionary activities (par. 145).

The astrological aspect of the Christ's birth is also directly alluded to in the story of the Magi who learned of an extraordinary birth from the stars (Matt. 2:1) and the aegis of the fishes is attested to by the rich fish symbolism in the gospels. Inasfar as Christ was regarded as the new eon, it would be obvious to anyone who had studied astrology that he was born as the first fish and died as the ram (par. 146).

Jung then speaks of many early representations of the sign of the fishes, sometimes swimming parallel, sometimes one vertical and one horizontal and often in opposite directions (par. 147).

Although there is no direct proof of a connection to the figure of Christ, the synchronicity of the appeareance of so many fish symbols and the beginning of our era is striking enough to justify our giving it our full attention. It is astonishing, when one comes to think of it, that the spring point should move into the fishes and then inaugurate a time when "fish" was used as a name for a God who became man, who was born as a fish and sacrificed as a ram, who had fishermen as disciples whom he wanted to become "fishers of men," who miraculously fed the multitude with fishes, who was himself eaten as a fish and whose followers were called little fishes. Here I would like to mention that Eucharistic plates with fish as well as bread depicted on them were found in the catacombs, and are therefore very early in date. There is no evidence whatever that the fish stories in the Synoptic gospels were disguised astrological myths. On the contrary, they appear quite naturally as just-so stories, a kind of synchronistic event with the beginning of the sign of the fishes (par. 148).

Jung ends the chapter with a reference to the time element as we move along the sign of the fishes, but as this is more clearly expressed in the beginning of the next chapter, we will postpone it until then.

VII

The Prophecies of Nostradamus

JUNG SAYS THAT THE COURSE OF OUR RELIGIOUS HISTORY and an essential part of our psychic development could have been more or less accurately predicted – as regards time and content – from the precession of the equinoxes through the constellation of the Fishes. An *enantiodromia* set in from the vertical Gothic striving toward the heights to a horizontal movement outwards, ushered in by the voyages of discovery and the rapidly increasing "conquest of nature." The vertical was cut across by the horizontal (one remembers that in many of the old representations of Pisces, one fish is vertical and the other horizontal), and man's spiritual development moved in what became increasingly obvious was an anti-Christian direction, leading to the present-day crisis whose outcome is still very dubious (par. 150).

With this background in mind, Jung then turns to Nostradamus. I shall only summarize this very briefly, partly for the reasons already mentioned and partly because although I have tried more than once to study Nostradamus, we two somehow do not click!

Yet one must admit it is exceedingly interesting that, in a letter to Henry II of France, dated June 27, 1558, he prophesies that, founded on astrological basis, the year 1792, more than two hundred years later, will see a greater persecution of the Christian Church than there ever was in Africa, though at the time "everyone will think it a renovation of the age" (par. 151).

Nostradamus may have based his own calculations on earlier authorities, but it is certainly striking that whereas an earlier prophecy said "1789" and Nostradamus said "1792," that both dates fall in the time of the French Revolution. The enthronement of the Goddess of Reason in Notre Dame de Paris was indeed (as Jung has often also elsewhere pointed out) a dramatic event which proved to be an anticipation of an increasingly anti-Christian trend and yet was hailed at the time by many as a "renovation of the age," exactly as Nostradamus prophesied two hundred and thirty years before. There was even a revolutionary calendar – with a new system of dating – begun in September 1792 (par. 156).

Great stress is laid on the north, both by Nostradamus and the earlier authorities. They would have been familiar with the idea of the north as the abode of the devil. This idea goes right back to the Old Testament where Jeremiah says: "From the north shall an evil wind break forth upon all the inhabitants of the land" (Jer. 1:14), and Isiah speaks of Lucifer as intending to exalt his throne above the stars of God and to sit on the mount of assembly in the far north (Isa. 14:12) (par. 157).

The Benedictine monk, Rhabanus Maurus (ninth century) says that the "north wind is the harshness of persecution" and "a figure of the old enemy." He adds that it is obvious that the north signifies the devil because it is said in Job: "He stretcheth out the north, over the empty space, and hangeth the earth upon nothing" (Job 26:7). Rhabanus Maurus interprets this as meaning that "God allows the devil to rule the minds of those who are empty of his grace" (par. 157).

Jung quotes St. Augustine and several other authorities who identify the north and the devil and adds that it is hardly surprising that Nostradamus and his predecessors warn us concerning "a usurper from the north" when they prophesy the coming of the Antichrist. Luther had promptly been greeted as the Antichrist, which is probably why Nostradamus speaks of "the second Antichrist" who is to appear after the year 1792. Jung just mentions that we should not forget how much capital the Nazis tried to make out of the idea that Hitler was completely the work of reformation which Luther left incomplete. (As Jung has often pointed out elsewhere, Nazi Germany was an example par excellence of the process of individuation *happening* unconsciously and automatically and therefore negatively.) (par. 159)

Jung ends the chapter by saying that, given the existing astrological data and the possibilities then extant of interpreting them, it was not difficult for Nostradamus to predict the imminent *enantiodromia* of the Christian eon; but by doing so he already stood himself in the anti-Christian phase and served as its mouthpiece. [The German is *stand er selber schon in der antichristlichen Phase drin* – literally translated, he thus stood already in the anti-Christian phase. The English translation "placed himself firmly" is misleading here, as it sounds as though Nostradamus did this *consciously* which was, of course, not the case. Now this is a very common intellectual error that arises from the prejudice that there is no unconscious which has a genuine effect upon us, but that we do everything consciously.]

[We can see this same process as one sees here in Nostradamus in ourselves if we look back on the time when we first came into contact with Jungian psychology. Our dreams then will show us how much our unconscious standpoint was changed, though our conscious lagged behind. It is often particularly clear in the transference, which can be in full bloom years before we realize it.]

VIII

The Historical Significance of the Fish

THE SHEPHERD AND THE LAMB PLAY, as we all know, an almost greater role in Christian symbolism than the fish. Shepherd, ram, and lamb symbolism coincides with the then-expiring eon of this period – Attis and Christ are *both* characterized as shepherds, rams, and fishes. The Poimen symbolism, however, has been so thoroughly investigated by Reitzenstein that Jung says he could add nothing illuminating to it, whereas the sources of the fish symbol are not only more copious, but the symbol itself – particularly in its dual aspects – gives rise to definite psychological questions that still call for elucidation (par. 162).

Jung then speaks of Christ's threatened birth and early childhood, a theme that is always connected with the birth of a hero, and points out pagan prototypes for this being connected with the fish, for instance, Leto and Python and Aphrodite and her son, who – when pursued – leaped into the Euphrates and were changed into fish, which connects the fish symbolism with mother and son. Moreover the Greeks identified Derceto-Atargatis and her son Ichthys with the constellation of Pisces (par. 163).

Jung here goes into the theme of the woman in Revelation who, while pregnant, was pursued by the dragon into the desert and also speaks of the description of the lamb with seven horns and seven eyes, a very bellicose animal and a great contrast to the meek lamb led to the slaughter (Rev. 5:6). Presumably the author of the Apocalypse was influenced by the idea of Christ having an opposite, a psychological shadow, with whom the triumphant Christ would unite, through an act of rebirth, at the end of time. The seven-horned ram is just about everything that Christ was not, yet he cannot be described as the Antichrist, a creation of the devil, and is by no means as irreconcilable with Christ as the latter. The duplication of the Christ figure, therefore, cannot be traced back to the lamb of the Apocalypse and is probably more due to the anti-Roman resentment felt by the Jewish Christians, who then fell back on the Old Testament God of vengeance (par. 164).

Jung then quotes examples showing the Jewish difficulties with the Messianic idea and sums up by saying that the weakness in this idea was probably on account of the split which in time developed into a complete polarity. The story in Job appears again in the Eighty-ninth Psalm, and Ibn Ezra tells of a great sage who was unable to read this psalm because it saddened him too much (par. 169).

There is then a piece which I found difficult but exceedingly interesting, concerning the relation of the God-image to the Self. I will attempt to give its gist in my own words. As the God-image always represents the highest psychic value, it is related to or even identical with the Self. Therefore any uncertainty about the God-image causes uneasiness in the relationship to the Self and, as this is very painful to us, we usually try to ignore it. But the ignored question is taken up in the unconscious and is answered by things like materialism, atheism, and the other isms, which then spread like wildfire. If no legitimate answer is given, or even seriously searched for, such results are unavoidable (par. 170).

[I will try to make this clearer by relating it to individual psychology. My own experience anyway goes to show that if a question or problem is constellated, and I shirk it, refuse its painful implications and repress it, the animus will immediately take over and fill me with beside-the-point opinions, until I feel completely out of myself and entirely disoriented. The worst of it is that by this time one has sometimes even successfully forgotten the *point de départ* and yet the only remedy that I know is to return to it, stand the pain and face the question to the best of one's ability. It is undoubtedly painful, yet – through the pain – one feels an instant sense of relief that the illusionary nonsense is over and that life once more makes sense, even if painful sense. The collective "bewilderment and confusion" that Jung describes here as a result of no adequate answer to our present uncertainty about the God-image exactly coincides with what I feel individually when I am not doing my best to find a conscious answer to some painful and difficult problem.]

Jung points out that the Christian answer of denying the reality of evil is no longer adequate in the world we live in today, so we are forced back on the early Christian prophecy of the Antichrist and on the speculations of the Gnostics and of Jewish mysticism, if we are to find a broad enough basis for our problem. The Gnostics – in contrast to the early fathers of the church – took evil very seriously, and Jewish mysticism went quietly on in its own way considering problematical depths which Christian writers were unfortunately doing their best to cover up (par. 170).

The dualistic aspect of the Christ figure is very evident in both the Gnostic and Jewish-Christian fields of thought, and Jung says he has dwelt on it because – through the symbol of the fish – Christ was assimilated into a world of ideas that may seem far removed from the gospels, a world of pagan origin and full of astrology. It is, however, an undeniable historical fact that Christ was born at the beginning of the age of the fishes and that Christ's birthplace was actually found by the Magi through the stars (par. 172).

Jung then quotes a lot more material, of which I want to stress only one idea. Saying that the fish was originally one and only later split into two, he refers to the fact that the fish goddesses were originally one and then gave birth to a fish son, thus bringing in the idea of mother and son. The mythological mothers were usually a danger to their sons and were devouring mothers (par. 173).

[I should like to point out here that though the devouring mother is not a Christian idea, Mary being thought of as almost as perfect as Christ, it would explain why Christ so often denied his mother, a fact which is often glossed over. He had to oppose her in order to live his life as a man, an aspect which, as far as I know, is usually ignored by the Church.]

After a good deal more material, Jung says that since the fishes also stand for mother and son, the tragedy of the son's early death is already implicit in the sign of the fishes. The astrological characteristics of the fish have all the essential components of the Christian myth: the cross (vertical and horizontal); the moral conflict and its splitting into Christ and Antichrist; the virgin birth; the classical mother-son tragedy; the danger at birth; and the saviour and healer. All this shows us that it is relevant to bring Christ as a fish into relationship with the eon then dawning, although there is no evidence that this connection was made at the time it happened (par. 177).

Among a good deal more further material, I should like just to mention the Syrian Apocalypse of Baruch, which says that Leviathan shall rise from the sea with the advent of the Messiah. We find a similar idea in Christian symbology where the crucifix is the bait with which God catches the Leviathan (Jung 1944, fig. 28). According to the same Apocalypse, Behemoth as well as Leviathan is a eucharistic food and, both here and at the beginning of the next chapter, Jung quotes very interesting excerpts referring to these animals as food for the end of time. Scheftelowitz is even of the opinion that the "very great and pure fish" mentioned in the Abercius inscription "is none other than the Leviathan" (par. 178).

[I found it particularly interesting here that Jung attributes the Jewish refusal of Christ as the Messiah to the split between Christ and Antichrist. The Jews had real justification, for Yahweh – as described in the Old Testament – is too much transformed into his opposite and not convincingly assimilated in the perfect figure of Christ. This would mean perhaps that – like Nostradamus – their unconscious moved a step on, into an age where Christ and

Satan have to come together, which might account partly for their difficulties in getting on with Christians and to some extent for the resentment that occasionally breaks out in Christian countries against them: the resentment would then be a projection of the Christians' own resentment that they cannot remain Jesus' little unconscious lambs but must themselves look for a union of opposites, including Christ's dark opposite.]

IX

The Ambivalence of the Fish Symbol

JUNG GOES ON WITH THE SYRIAN APOCALYPSE of Baruch (which one can find in Charles (1985)) where it says that the time preceding the coming of the Messiah falls into twelve parts and the Messiah will come in the twelfth. As a division of time, this points to the twelve signs of the zodiac, of which the twelfth is the fishes. The twelfth is thus the end and the beginning. The Leviathan will then rise out of the sea. As the Behemoth is undoubtedly a land animal, the *two* sea monsters referred to in Baruch must be a duplication of the Leviathan, and the latter is also alluded to there as male and female. Now in Job, and all the earlier texts, the Leviathan is only one. Then he was the opposite of the most high God but – as he splits into two – God is, so to speak, relieved of his own inner conflict and can now watch the conflict of two hostile brothers *outside* himself. We often see this split in the shadow in modern dreams, especially where the ego personality is unaware of components it would know. If we apply this psychological experience to the mythological material we are discussing, then we could suggest that God's monstrous antagonist produces a double because the God-image is incomplete. Carrying this further – with Christ as the other fish – we could postulate that it was the human element that was previously lacking in the God-image, as indeed we know from other sources (par. 181).

Jung goes on with many examples of an ambivalent attitude to the fish. In Egypt, for instance, it was generally held to be unclean and negative, yet among many positive opposites, I mention a painting on a late Hellenistic sarcophagus, where there is a fish hovering over the mummy instead of the usual soul bird. It is even clear in the painting that this fish is one of three most abominated fishes, said to have eaten the phallus of Osiris after he had been dismembered by Set. These fish were sacred to Typhon (Set) who represents the "passionate, impulsive, irrational and truculent" part of the soul, so it is really interesting that it should be represented on this sarcophagus as the soul image hovering over the mummy (par. 187).

Jung goes on with Horus and Set, the former a god of the day and the latter of the night and therefore enemies. This pair of gods (latent opposites contained in Osiris) is an interesting parallel to Behemoth and Leviathan in relation to Yahweh. But both work together when it comes to helping the one god, Osiris, to reach the heavenly quarternity (par. 187).

In Arab tradition, the region around the pole is seen in the form of a fish. Ezekiel's vision of God came from the north, in spite of the fact that the north is usually regarded as the birthplace of all evil. Such coincidence of the opposites is normal in all primitive conceptions of God, for he is then just taken for granted. But when people begin to reflect *consciously*, the coincidence of the opposites becomes a tough nut to crack, and we try to avoid the problem in every way we can. The position of the devil in Christianity is highly unsatisfactory but when such gaps are left in the collective dominants, they will certainly be compensated from the unconscious. The alchemists, however, aimed at bottom at a more or less conscious restoration of a primitive God-image and thus were able to propound paradoxes, which shock us by their frankness but which are yet contained in the Christian religion but never brought together in consciousness. Who speaks of hellfire, for instance, in the same breath as the *privatio boni?* Yet both are Christian doctrines (par. 189).

Jung says here: "What they were aiming at was a more or less conscious restoration of the primitive God-image. Hence they were able to propound paradoxes as shocking as that of God's love glowing in the midst of hell-fire" (par. 191; see also Jung 1944, par. 446).

I worked for a short time with Emma Jung, and something which I learned from her has been a tremendous help to me ever since in relating to negative emotions. She had a tremendous belief in something that came out of her own experience. She said that if you had a dreadful depression, or became very angry, or had any negative emotion that one usually tries to repress or evade, her idea was to treat such emotion, as far as you could, as a friend or an animal and to relate to it and eventually get it to tell you why it felt that way. Therefore if you have a terrible depression, instead of working it off with a drink or a walk or something, speak to it, relate to it, and say "I suppose you have your reasons?" I have got so much out of this technique, and I think when the alchemists speak of God's love glowing out of hellfire it gives something of a picture of the paradox of being able to stand one's negative emotion without running away from it.

When we think of Nostradamus's "king of the North," we should not forget what a paradox the north is in the ancient writers: it is the seat of the highest gods and of Lucifer. Particularly relevant is Bernard de Clairvaux's cry to Lucifer: "And dost thou strive perversely towards the North? The more thou dost hasten toward the heights, the more speedily shalt thou go down to thy setting" (par. 120).

Here I would like to comment that really the idea that gave rise to such fury after *Answer to Job* was the presentation of God as, so to speak, the prototype, as the development in every individual. In the individual there is this split into two figures if you are not conscious where you could be conscious, and this is exactly what Jung showed in the book for, if you remember, he so often said that if Yahweh had only listened to his Sophia, the universal knowledge within himself, he could have been conscious that he also had a dark side. If you watch dreams, it is most interesting when the shadow appears as two figures, if you can manage to find out the makeup of the two, for one will be nearer to consciousness than the other. The latter will be more difficult to detach and may be contaminated with archetypal material.

The whole question is very interesting but very difficult. You know that in a dream there appear very often not one but two shadow figures. If you think about them, of how you feel to them and of their most outstanding qualities and of what they mean to you, you will probably find that one is nearer to you than the other and that you know more about this one. On the other hand, Jung says that a duplication of any figure is an indication that it is just coming to the surface and looks like two when it is really one. If you take the idea of the Behemoth and Leviathan figures in Job, they are the dark side of God. When Job is very unhappy and tells God of his unhappiness, God just boasts of the wonderful animals he has made, and Leviathan and Behemoth carry God's split-off shadow. If I understand it correctly, the shadow that is first thrown out is later duplicated when the two fight each other like a pair of hostile brothers, and that would represent the stage of becoming more objective, for it can be watched as a conflict. When I was having enormous difficulty in seeing my shadow because it was so unacceptable to me, I dreamed of two women who, though they were doing their utmost, could not understand each other, but then they danced, and by that they could each go their own way, just occasionally meeting and coming closer together. I think that at first one does not at all see that one's shadow has anything to do with oneself and that the next step is to see it as an unacceptable pair of opposites fighting with each other, from which you can get the idea that you also have these unacceptable figures in you, which makes a terrible split, for there are two women in you, or two shadows, who know nothing of each other. At first this seemed like mere words to me, and I never had any success in dealing with my shadow until I got the idea of the possibility of a synchronization as in the dance. The duplication, as I see it, has to do with objectification, but that is my own experience and does not come out of *Aion*.

X

The Fish in Alchemy

The Medusa

Before beginning this chapter, I would like to remind you of what Jung says in the introduction to *Psychology and Alchemy* about the relation of alchemy to Christianity, for though it is constantly implied, it is never expressed as clearly in *Aion*. He says: "The point is that alchemy is rather like an undercurrent to the Christianity that ruled on the surface. It is to this surface as the dream is to consciousness, and just as the dream compensates the conflicts of the conscious mind, so alchemy endeavours to fill the gaps left by the Christian tension of opposites" (Jung 1944, par. 25).

The chapter falls into three parts and is mainly material. It is therefore very difficult to summarize. I shall try to be very brief, leaving you to fill in the gaps.

The "Allegoriae super librum Turbae" is our earliest source of alchemical fish symbolism; probably this material comes from before the eleventh century. The fish, in the earliest reference, is "a round fish" that contains a fatness, a wonderful virtue. If cooked, it begins to shine, presumably a kind of jellyfish (par. 194). Probably the author was influenced by Pliny, who speaks of a fish that was so hot that everything it touched was consumed by fire (par. 197). Pliny mentions the *stella marina* in the same breath. Maybe zoological distinctions were not important to Pliny, but anyway the medieval alchemists seized on the idea, and Nicholas Caussin regarded the animal as a starfish and endowed it with the quality of generating so much heat that he compares it to the "inextinguishable power of true love" (par. 197).

Picinellus goes even further and – with still more elaborate amplification – compares it with the fire of the Holy Ghost and to the miracle at Pentecost. The miraculous fact that water does not extinguish its fire reminds Picinellus of "the action of divine grace" which sets hearts on fire although they are drowned in a "sea of sins." For the same reason the fish means divine love, and he quotes the Song of Solomon: "Many waters cannot quench love, neither can the floods drown it" (Song of Sol. 8:7). It spreads a radiance about itself from the moment of its birth.

As we see from the reference to the Song of Solomon, this starfish also refers to profane love, and Picinellus even says that this starfish is the "hieroglyph of a lover's heart" whose passion cannot be extinguished by the whole sea whether his love is divine or profane, and he also calls it the "concupiscentia" and "the spark of lechery" (par. 199).

Jung points out how strange it is that the medieval symbolists give diametrically opposed interpretations of one and the same symbol apparently without becoming conscious of the dangerous fact that they are implying the identity of the opposites. He brings many more examples – mainly concerned with the fire – but I will leave you to read these for yourselves. He also brings a most interesting modern dream which leads to the lysis of the dreamer seeing, in the center of a circular pool, in the depths of a dark wood, "a pearly organism about eighteen inches in diameter, that emitted a faint light. It was a jellyfish" (par. 208). Now the twenty-year-old student who had the dream was under no psychological influence, so the cropping up of this symbol in a modern dream (and it is by no means unique) is very interesting.

The Fish

Up until now the fish under discussion has been a round fish, a kind of jellyfish, not really zoologically a fish at all. But by the sixteenth century, there is no doubt in the texts that a real fish is meant, and it then becomes clear that "the round fish" in the "Aenigmata" was regarded as a real fish in alchemistic tradition.

A round and transparent fish of a peculiar kind is described in the *Cyranides* (a medieval text on animals, stones, plants, etc.). It lived in the sea around Syria and Libya and had three stones, two in its head and one in the third vertebra of its tail. These stones were said to be powerful and were much sought after as love charms. This stone is twin and twofold: the one is opaque and black but the other, though also black, is brilliant and shines like a mirror. "This is the stone which many seek for it is the dragon's stone" (par. 128). This stone was already known to Pliny and to the medieval alchemists. It was reputed to be precious. Ruland – in his *Lexicon* – asserts that he has seen such stones, blue or black in color (in another place he calls them white). Again we have the opposites, and the cinedian stone reminds us of the lapis which signifies the polarity and union of the opposites. We have already seen that the alchemical fish symbol points ultimately to the archetype of the Self (par. 216).

We then come to perhaps the most interesting fish in alchemy and now it becomes a verifiable vertebrate fish known to zoology: the *echineis remora* (*remora* is the Latin for "delay"). It belongs to the mackerel family and is characterized by a large, flat, oval-shaped sucker on the top of its head in the place of the dorsal fin. It can attach itself by means of this sucker to a large fish or a ship and thus let itself be transported round the world (par. 217).

A seventeenth-century text, by an anonymous French author, goes into great detail about this fish. Unwarrantably condensed, he says that this very small and lonely fish is what is indispensable for the philosophical work and it is shut up in "that deep mid region of the great universal sea" (par. 218). One must know where it is, for the fish is small and the ocean vast. He even says that it is no more difficult to draw the moon down from the sky than to find this fish. Yet those who know the "hidden secret of the wise" can catch this little fish naturally, easily and speedily, although it itself is able to hold back the proud vessels of the great sea which is the spirit of the world. He goes on to explain that it must be caught in accordance with nature and by means of the "magnet of the wise" and then speaks of its transformation and the effect it can have when properly prepared (par. 218).

Jung always says that the "theoria" of the alchemists is their teaching – what can be learned from books and what books can give. He has said more than once that the only way that one can really test one's doctrine, that is, what one has learned, is on one's own figures. He has remarked that he was not impressed by the number of people who came to any of his pupils, what impressed him was if he saw that their own figures were listening to them and if they were making progress with their own shadow, animus, or anima. I remember that when I went through the usual "measles" of wanting to become an analyst, a "measles" which everyone gets whether they later become analysts or not, Jung pointed out to me that I should have to go to England if I wanted to analyze. Shortly afterwards I had a dream of analyzing a woman who was clearly my shadow, who said that if I wanted to know the best preparation for becoming an analyst it would be by analyzing my own internal figures because if they listened to me they got the right idea, and if they did not, then I would make no impression on others. When I did begin to do analyzing, there was nothing I wanted to do less – when one wants something, it does not come, but give it up and it will come whether you like it or not.

As regards the fact that this little fish can stop the proud frigates of the sea, we hear from Pliny that this little fish sucked itself fast onto the rudder of Caligula's boat and brought it to a standstill. After this journey, on his return to Rome, Caligula was murdered by his soldiers. Therefore, as Pliny points out, it was an omen. And the same happened to Mark Anthony before his naval battle with Augustus in which Anthony was killed. Pliny cannot marvel enough at the mysterious powers of Echineis. Maybe he influenced the alchemists so much that they identified their "round fish" with the *echineis remora* (par. 223).

Jung goes on to point out that fish also come in the writings of Ripley where, together with the birds, they bring the stone, just as they point the way to the kingdom of heaven in the *Oxyrhynchus Sayings of Jesus*. They also appear in Lambsprinck's symbols as the fishes of the zodiac, moving in opposite directions and symbolizing the secret substance (par. 224).

The Fish Symbol of the Catharists

In the third section of "The Fish in Alchemy," Jung turns to the archives of the Inquisition and unearths a most interesting Catharist document. (The Cathars are one of the sects that began in the twelfth century at the time when Joachim of Flora was announcing his era of the Holy Ghost. It was definitely heretical, in contrast to alchemy itself.) (par. 225)

This text deals with a revelation said to have been given by Christ to his favorite disciple, John. John asked about the condition of Satan before his fall and was told of his splendor, marred by the fact that he wanted to be like God, and, with this end in view, Satan descended to the earth, which was still covered with water, and found two fish yoked together like oxen for ploughing from sunset to sunrise, that is, from west to east. The vision goes on with Satan, who was stopped by fire (his Osob) from going deeper, returning to heaven. But he was soon being cast out from there on account of his arrogance. He was allowed a week, however, in which to create the earth on the model of Genesis (par. 225).

Jung remarks that the idea that Satan, not God, created the earth was very prevalent in several sects at that time. But the important theme for us in this text is the two fish, yoked together like oxen for ploughing. One must remember St. Augustine's interpretation of the two fish in the miracle of feeding the five thousand to understand this symbol. The two fish represented the kingly and priestly power to Augustine, because they survived the turbulence of the multitude, as fish survive the storms of the sea. Not that the two fish in our text were those in the miracle, but because we see that fish were regarded as ruling powers. As this is a heretical text, it probably goes back to the idea of the double sonship, reported by Epiphanius of the Ebionites: God's two sons, Sataniel and Christ (par. 228).

It is particularly interesting that Satan found these fish *before the creation*, so we may assume that they were thought of as the fish in the zodiac. Cosmogonic myths are at bottom symbols for the coming of consciousness (as you know from Dr. von Franz's lectures on the creation myths) so these fish would characterize the ascendant, the moment of the world's birth. Giving more confirmatory material, Jung sums up by saying: "Expressed psychologically, therefore, the two fishes which the devil found on the primeval waters would signify the newly arisen world of consciousness" (par. 230). (I remind you that the sign of the fishes is the twelfth sign of the zodiac, an end and a beginning.)

The fish being yoked like oxen is especially interesting. Wherever man ploughs virgin earth, he has conquered a piece of primal soil. That is to say, the sign of the fishes will rule this world and, working by the astrological destiny of *man*, will mold his consciousness. Most things begin in the east, but this ploughing begins in the west. This motif is fairly frequent in alchemy, the work begins with the *nigredo*, the descent into the unconscious, and ploughs its way to the east, the rising sun of consciousnes (par. 231).

The Catharist sect began soon after the turning point in the sign of the fishes, from Christ to Antichrist. But we do not know if the allusions in the texts are a conscious reference to astrological ideas or rather a synchronistic product of the unconscious. We know well enough from myths and fairy tales that the unconscious continually produces such things (par. 233).

Jung then goes – more clearly than before – into the sequence of events in the sign of the Fishes, and says that the new world began at about the turning point, 1000 A.D., and its advent was soon proclaimed by all the sects that sprang up at the same time Joachim of Flora announced the new era of the Holy Ghost. Medieval alchemy began at much the same time, and both – especially the idea of the era of the Holy Ghost – led to the Reformation, which, in its turn, led to the enthroning of the goddess of reason in Notre Dame de Paris and the victory of the natural sciences, leading on to the increasingly devilish development of our own day and to the far-reaching "evaporation of Christianity under the assaults of rationalism, intellectualism, materialism and so-called 'realism'" (par. 235).

Jung ends the chapter with some very interesting dreams of a silver and gold fish, but I will not attempt to summarize them or their interpretations as they need studying in their entirety. It is another case of the old fish symbolism appearing spontaneously in the unconscious of a young woman who knew nothing of the historical symbol of the fish (par. 236).

The two fish, harnessed like oxen and found by Satan of all figures, fascinates me in all its detail. It was said to be a revelation by Christ to John while he rested on the Lord's bosom and it assigns a more positive role to his opposite than we often find. True, Satan falls from heaven in the orthodox way, as the church teaches that Christ saw him do, but not only does he find the two fishes – yoked together for a common purpose – but he also creates the world. The latter view is quite common, it is true, so it is only interesting that this Catharist document puts it into the mouth of Christ. But the two fish – working together for a purpose – reminds us of the way Horus and Set worked together for the purpose of helping the *one* god, Osiris, to reach the heavenly quaternity, and this is very rare in Christian documents, even heretical ones.

The fact that Satan is the one who finds these united fish seems to me especially significant in view of the fact that the story originated in the time of the second fish, that is, of the Antichrist, and seems to me to contain a grain of hope that we can very well do with in these dark days. Namely, that there seems – according to this text – a hope of uniting the opposites; even though these days are ruled by the dark brother, in fact, it is *he* who leads down to it, which makes it seem possible that the devilish days we live in may yet lead to a union of the opposites.

XI

The Alchemical Interpretation of the Fish

THIS CHAPTER BEGINS WITH TURNING BACK to the Echineis fish. We learn in a footnote – I just mentioned this fact before – that Du Cange in his *Glossarium*, says that its second name, *remora* (Latin for "delay"), comes from the fact that this small fish can hold a ship stationary even in a storm. In the point of view of the alchemists, the adept has, as it were, to win this magnetic secret from the fish and then use it in his work of preparing the *lapis* or *filius philosophorum* (par. 239).

Our anonymous French author insists that the "magnet of the wise" that is to draw up this wonder-working fish *can be taught*. The content of this secret alchemistic "doctrine" or "theory" is the real arcanum of alchemy: the discovery or production of the *prima materia*. As we know it has a thousand names, the alchemists talk about it a lot but tell us little or nothing. Presumably there was no such concrete substance and nothing that the intellect could grasp (par. 240).

One on its long list of names is magnesia, though not of course chemical magnesia. It is closely associated with the magnet, not only by the sound of its name but also in meaning. Rosinus, for instance, speaks of the "lapis animalis" (the animate stone) which is able to feel or perceive the influence of the magnesia and magnet. Many authors are quoted, of which I will only mention Dorn, who speaks of a spirit hidden within the magnetic stone because we cannot see its powers of attraction with our eyes. This numinous effect of the incomprehensible power of magnetism on our forefathers is well described by St. Augustine who says that "a cold shiver" went through him when he saw it for the first time (*vehementer inhorrui*) (par. 243).

Like the heavenly dew and water, the magnet symbolizes the alchemistic doctrine itself, therefore we hear that it can be taught. Dorn says that the Gentiles say "that nature seeks after a nature like to itself, and rejoices in its own nature," an allusion to the well-known axiom of Democritus: "Nature rejoices in nature; nature subdues nature; nature rules over nature" (par. 244).

The double hermaphroditic nature is then illustrated in several excerpts, and Jung says that obviously a difference must be made between two categories of symbols: those that refer to an extrapsychical substance (or its metaphysical equivalent), such as *serpens mercurialis, spiritus, veritas*, and so on; and those denoting chemical preparations, such as the solvents, or their "philosophical" equivalent, the *theoria* or miraculous effect on matter (par. 246).

Pernety describes this confusion when he says: "It must not be supposed that this magnet is the common magnet. They [the alchemists] have given it this name only because of its natural sympathy with their steel" and so on (par. 247).

In Dorn it appears in a similar way: the *veritas*, which for him is hidden in natural things, is – at the same time – a "moral" concept. This truth is a medicine which needs no medicament, being itself an incorrupt medicament, and which can restore things to what they were before their corruption. "The Philosophers, through a kind of divine inspiration, knew that this virtue and heavenly vigor can be freed from its fetters: not by its contrary … but by its like …." And later: "by peace rather than war" (par. 248).

Dorn, Jung says later, was the first thinker to recognize with the utmost clarity the extraordinary dilemma of alchemy: the arcane substance is one and the same, whether it is found "inside" man or outside him. The alchemistic procedure takes place within and without, and nobody who does not understand how to free the truth in himself will ever be able to do so outside, in the physical opus (par. 249).

Dorn comes to realize more and more the fundamental importance of self-knowledge. What you expect outside must first be applied to yourself. We can never get rid of doubt except by experiment, and we cannot make this experiment on a better place than on ourselves. Therefore Dorn exhorts the adepts: "Learn from within thyself to know all that is in heaven and on earth" (par. 250).

Such knowledge is obviously not knowledge of the nature of the ego but objective knowledge of the nature of the Self. Jung says, in "Notes on Lectures given at the Eidgenössische Technische Hochschule, Zürich":

> As to this self knowledge, this real penetrating knowledge of our own being, do not make the mistake of thinking that it means seeing through the ego. To understand the ego is child's play, but to see through the Self is something totally different. The real difficulty lies in recognising the unknown. No one need remain ignorant of the fact that he is striving for power, that he wants to become very rich, that he would be a tyrant if he had the chance, that he is pleasure seeking, envious of other people, and so on. Everyone *can* know such things of him or herself, because they are mere ego knowledge. But Self knowledge is something completely different, it is learning to know of the things which are unknown. (1960, p. 72)

It is this objective knowledge of the Self that Dorn means when he says: "No one can know himself unless he knows *what*, and not *who* he is" (par. 252).

This difference between what and who is crucial because "who" is a personal pronoun and refers to the ego, whereas "what" is neuter and refers to an object. That means the psyche itself is the unknown, unprejudiced object that still needs investigation (par. 252).

You see until one has some idea of what the "what" in oneself is, one can be caught by it quite blindly as, for instance, happened to the Germans with the concentration camps. If only the majority had stopped to think what they were doing! But because they had no idea of the "what" in the human soul, both in the dark and light aspect, they simply let themselves be caught and possessed by the dark side. I am reading *The Diary of a Young Girl* by Anne Frank. She was in hiding in Amsterdam for two years before she was caught and put in the concentration camp at Auschwitz and afterwards at Belsen. The book gives you some idea of the incredible thing which caught people who could take a harmless girl like that and feel it was their duty to destroy her. That really is the reason why we have to know the "what" in us.

This sixteenth-century alchemist, with his *quis* (who) and *quod* (what) has put his finger clearly on something that psychologists are still stumbling over today. It recalls the opening of Ignatius of Loyola's *Fundamentum*: "Man was created to praise, do reverence to and serve God our Lord and thereby to save his soul" (par. 252).

If we translate this sentence from theological language to psychological, it would roughly mean: man's consciousness was created so that it might recognize its descent from a higher unity, observe and pay due respect to his source, execute its commands intelligently and responsibly, and thus give the total psyche an optimum degree of life and development (par. 253).

The paraphrase is, and is meant to be, rational and reasonable, for the modern mind no longer understands our nearly two-thousand-year-old theological language, with the result that, to a great extent, it is long since replaced by lip service or indifference (par. 254).

We prefer to bury our talents (Luke 19:12) and not to understand that evil is at work everywhere, though this is incredibly infantile, for the more unconscious we are, the more the devil drives us. It is the inner, unconscious connection with the dark side that makes it so fatally and incredibly easy for the mass man to commit the most appalling crimes without for a moment thinking what he is doing. Only ruthless self-knowledge on a wide scale can save us from a fatal result (par. 255).

Sixteenth-century Dorn expresses the crucial importance of self-knowledge particularly clearly, but we find it much earlier in the literature, in Morienus Romanus, for instance, in the seventh to eighth century and in *Rosinus ad Sarratantam Episcopum*, one of the oldest Arabic translations of a lost Zosimos text. The latter text is rather a difficult passage which I will leave you to study for yourselves; it describes the situation as regards the Self very exactly. It is small – smallest of the small – and easily overlooked. It needs help and must be perceived, protected, and, as it were, built up by the conscious mind but over against this it has always been there and is the *spiritus rector* of our fate. It is far greater than the ego which is always contained in it, yet in this world it is dependent on our *knowledge* of it (par. 256).

Other passages from the old pre-Dorn masters are quoted, amazingly parallel descriptions to our own *experience* of the Self; or is it amazing, for the archetype is naturally the same everywhere if one is able to experience it? The trouble is that one needs enough knowledge to be able to assimilate the experience when it comes or else it simply gives rise to neurotic symptoms. This is why it is so vitally important to tell children fairy stories and legends and for grownups to study the religious dogmas, because these things are symbols and act as instruments to bring such experience into consciousness where it can then be interpreted and assimilated. When this does not happen, the energy flows off into conscious contents and intensifies them to pathological proportions, and we succumb to phobias, intellectual perversions, and the like (par. 259).

The alchemist, having no concept of the collective unconscious, was always confused as to where the Self was – inside or out – and many alchemists exteriorize it in the traditional way. Dorn gets round the paradox as follows: after saying that the "incorrupt medicament can only be found in heaven," he adds,

"No man can generate in himself but [only] in that which is like him, which is from the same [heaven]" (par. 262).

Dorn means just the same as the Indians when they speak of the personal and universal Atman. Today, we should call it the unconscious and be able to distinguish between a personal unconscious, that can be recognized in our own shadow, and an impersonal or collective unconscious in ourselves, that can be recognized as the archetypal symbol of the Self.

When Dorn says that it is only possible to unite the opposites in the stone when one has done so in oneself, he is describing the process of individuation exactly. He realized the identity of the lapis with the transformed man when he exclaimed: "Transmute yourselves from dead stones into living philosophical stones." He also speaks of this truth shining in us but not of us; we should not seek it in ourselves but in the image of God which itself *is in us* (par. 264).

Jung ends the chapter by saying how remarkable it is that Dorn, who expresses himself so much more clearly than his successor, Jacob Boehme, should have remained virtually unknown until today. He thus shared the fate of Hermetic philosophy (alchemy) in general, which remains for most people a book closed with seven seals. Yet this book *must* be opened if we are to understand the present day, for alchemy – and not scholasticism – is the mother of the essential substance of modern scientific thinking (par. 266).

XII

Background to the Psychology of Christian Alchemical Symbolism

THIS CHAPTER BEGINS WITH THE STATEMENT that "Mater Alchimia" could serve as a name for a whole epoch. Alchemy began almost with the Christian era and gave birth in the sixteenth and seventeenth centuries to the age of science and was forthwith forgotten. But every mother is first a daughter, and alchemy was the daughter of Gnosticism which – with the help of Greek philosophy, the mythologies of Asia Minor and Jewish Cabalism – attempted to synthesize the physical and mystical aspects into a unitary vision of the world. If this had succeeded, our world would not have split into two parallel points of view as it has today, where neither even attempts or wants to know anything of the other (par. 267).

This split was visible – already in the eighteenth century – in the rift between faith and knowledge. Faith lacked experience and science omitted the soul, ignoring the very existence of the psyche. Our Christian doctrine is indeed a highly differentiated symbol of the psyche but it excludes nature. Therefore there have always been undercurrents (like alchemy) that have tried to investigate the empirical side of nature, from within and without (par. 268).

Theology continues using a language that has become incomprehensible to the great majority today. The word *dogma* has even acquired an unpleasant nuance and is frequently used to emphasize the rigidity of a prejudice; it has largely lost its meaning as a symbol for an unknowable, yet actual, fact. Until the recent declaration of the *Assumptio Mariae,* it was hardly discussed, even in theological circles, a sure sign that the symbol is withering. Many people search for a substitute in the East, India, for instance. But although the Indian symbols formulate the unconscious just as well as the Christian, they do not express our spiritual past but their own. Therefore, though we can learn a lot from India, it cannot express our own stored-up past, so we shall never reach our roots that way, for we are rooted in nearly two thousand years of Christianity. In certain parts of Europe, it is true, this dwindles down to not much more than five hundred years, and then we reach pagan times and the Germanic myths (as the last war demonstrated only too clearly) (par. 270).

No doubt the spreading of Christianity among barbarian people favored a certain rigidity in the dogma, as we can see more clearly in Islam, which became both rigid and fanatical. This takes a very different course in the East, where Buddha was peacefully reassimilated by Hinduism in less than a millenium (par. 272).

We cannot take over Eastern forms of thought without uprooting ourselves, for we are rooted in Christian soil, and though this is alarmingly thin in some places, we then have to deal with our own original paganism and cannot side step this with a leap to the East (par. 273).

We find some of these pagan currents in alchemy which – reaching its summit in the sixteenth and seventeenth centuries – then apparently disappeared, and science led in the nineteenth century to materialism and in the twentieth to so-called "realism" whose end is not yet in sight. However much we hate to see it or admit it, the church is a helpless bystander, for – though her message is still effective – she does not use the language of the present but parrots sacrosanct words hallowed by age, regardless of whether she is understood or not. If St. Paul had used the language and myths of the Minoan Age in order to preach the gospel to the Athenians, what success would he have had? The language the church uses was coined in an age when people had no difficulty at all believing in miracles and had no modern knowledge, to say nothing of skepticism, to deal with. Every schoolboy today knows more of the ways of nature than all Pliny's volumes of natural history put together, yet the church goes on speaking in images that look deceptively familiar and yet are miles away from a modern man's conscious understanding. It will have to change its language if there is to be any hope of its essential meaning remaining effective (par. 274).

The bridge from the dogma to the inner experience of the individual has broken down, and we must face that fact. The faith of the man of antiquity and of the medieval Christian never ran counter to the *consensus gentium* (general opinion) but was supported by it. All that has changed radically in the last three hundred years. But have theological circles made any attempt to keep pace with this fact (par. 276)?

There is great danger that the new wine will burst the old bottles and that we shall repeat the mistake of the Reformation of throwing away everything we do not understand (par. 277).

Many people are surprised that Jung, as a doctor and psychologist, lays such stress on the dogma. But the same reasons that caused the alchemist to insist on his *theoria* forced Jung to look carefully at the dogma, namely the need to reach the roots of the hypothesis with which we experiment. The alchemist's doctrine consists in the quintessence of the symbolism of unconscious processes, just as the dogma is a concentration or distillation of the so-called "history of salvation," namely, the myth of divine being and doing since primeval days. In order to understand the alchemist's doctrine, we must return to the individual, as well as Christian dogma, and it is really vital for us to do so – we must *first* consider the myths of Asia Minor, which are the foundation of Christianity, and mythology in general as an expression of the general disposition of man, which Jung has called the collective unconscious (par. 278).

Myths and fantasies express unconscious processes and to study them reanimates the unconscious and begins to reestablish the connection between conscious and unconscious. It is disastrous when these two separate, and they can never reunite without a *tertium quod non datur*, a living symbol. For this reason the ancients compared the symbol to water – as, for instance, yang and yin united in Tao often represented as a "valley spirit," the winding course of a river. The church's symbol is the *aqua doctrinae* (the water of the doctrine), as alchemy's is their "divine water" whose double aspect is represented by Mercurius. This symbolic water is healing and renewing everywhere – whether it be the Christian baptismal water, Tao, or the alchemistic elixir, showing the therapeutic character of its mythological background. And in psychology we also know that there is a moral problem of the opposites at the bottom of every neurosis that can never be solved rationally but only by something superior to both sides: a symbol (par. 280).

The problem of the integration of the unconscious can only be solved by continuing along the lines laid down by history, but that presupposes a continuity in the development. The present tendency toward destruction – that is, letting the whole of tradition fall into the unconscious – may indeed interrupt the normal development with a barbaric interval of several hundred years. Where the idea of a Marxist utopia has won out, this has taken place already. And a predominantly scientific and technical education – which is characteristic of the United States – can bring about a turning back of the spiritual values and thus considerably increase the psychic dissociation. Loss of roots and lack of tradition just ask for neurosis and thus prepare the ground for a mass hysteria. Something (a kind of collective therapy) has to be used for collective hysteria and then individual liberty vanishes and terrorization begins (par. 282).

Jung then sums up the foregoing and says he has tried to show the kind of psychic matrix into which the Christ figure was spontaneously assimilated. Had there not been an affinity (a magnet!) between the figure of the Redeemer and certain contents of the unconscious, the human mind would never have seen the light in Christ and been so passionately gripped by it (par. 283).

It was the noncanonical symbol of the fish that led us down into this matrix, that is, it enabled us to experience the unknown sphere of the archetypes where the latter unceasingly change their names and garments, and we can only try to learn something of their hidden nucleus by circumambulation. The lapis, with its thousand names, is not Christ but it is his parallel in the subjective realm, and therefore it helps us to realize what he means in subjective experience (par. 284).

The fish symbol represents a spontaneous assimilation of the figure of Christ as he appears in the Gospels and is, as it were, a symptom of how he was received by the unconscious. The patristic allegory of the crucifix, as the bait to catch the Leviathan, is very characteristic: a fish has been caught and drawn up from the depths, attracted by the figure of Christ. But Christ himself? He also is hailed as Ichthys (fish), and this suggests that he also had come up out of the depths. The fish symbol, therefore, forms a bridge between the historical Christ and the psychic nature of man, where the archetype of the redeemer is at home. Christ thus became an inner experience (par. 285).

We have seen that the alchemistic symbolism of the fish leads in a direct line to the *lapis*, in psychological language, to the Self. We thus have a new symbol in place of the fish: the psychological concept of human wholeness (par. 286).

[Here – for I found this last sentence difficult to understand, particularly in the English – I would like to remind you that the symbol is always the best possible expression for an unknown fact beyond our comprehension, so when it comes to a new symbol, once again we are trying to express the inexpressible.]

Jung says that just as much or as little as the fish is Christ, so much or so little the Self is the Deity. They are both corresponding expressions and inner experiences. The idea of human totality is, as it were, a new assimilation of Christ in the psychic matrix, or a further realization of the son of God. This time it does not take a theriomorphic form but is expressed as a concept, as a "philosophical" symbol. This fact points to an increase in consciousness, over against the dumb and unconscious fish (par. 286).

XIII

Gnostic Symbols of the Self

THE TWO LAST CHAPTERS ARE THE LONGEST in the book and perhaps the most important. I have to shorten them very disagreeably. Chapter XIII is divided into no less than eight subdivisions, all of which would merit the time for a chapter.

PART 1

The first part begins by explaining that, as all recognizing is a kind of re-recognizing, it is to be expected that the gradual development, which we have been considering, would have been prefigured and anticipated at the beginning of our era. We find this already in Gnosticism, to which we must now turn our attention (par. 287).

The idea of the magnet, for instance, which we considered in connection with the *echineis remora* fish and the lapis in alchemy, is to be found three times in Hippolytus's *Elenchos*. First, it is found as water in the doctrine of the *Naassenes*. This is the water of the Euphrates – the critical fourth river of paradise – which has the same magnetic qualities as the *aqua doctrinae* which opens the way to perfecting every nature in its individuality and thus makes the human being also whole (par. 288).

In the *Peratic* doctrine, it is the "Son," symbolized by the serpent, that has the magnetic effect. The serpent is an equivalent of the fish: the Redeemer is a fish because he rose from unknown depths and a serpent because Christ is more authentic than the fish (that is, it can be found in an authentic logion); where the fish just appears in pictorial representations on the monuments and early utensils, the latter seems to have been more popular with the early Christians. Theriomorphic symbols are very common in dreams, and it is important for psychotherapy to realize that they depict the degree of unconsciousness: a warm-blooded animal represents something much nearer to consciousness than something cold-blooded or even invertebrate (par. 290).

In the *Sethian* doctrine, the magnetic attraction is attributed to the Logos. Here we find a very close parallel to the alchemistic *divisio* and *separatio*. The result of the unmixing is that everything can now hasten to its "own place" and to what is akin to it. The Logos is symbolized by a ray of light, or minute spark, in the dark water below. Hippolytus says that this spark or ray of light "having received from the teaching and learning its proper place, hastens to the Logos, which comes from above in the form of a slave ... more [quickly] than iron [flies] to the magnet" (par. 292).

Thus the three magnetic agents are *water*, an inanimate and passive substance; *serpent*, an animate and autonomous creature; and *logos*, a philosophical idea. Evidently these three symbols are all attempts to describe the incomprehensible, incarnated God. All three are phenomena of assimilation and are numinous themselves and therefore partly autonomous. Had such phenomena never appeared, it would have shown that Christ's annunciation had not taken effect. In other words, such symbols show that the historical appearance of the Christ figure awoke contents that were lying dormant in man's unconscious and attracted them as a magnet. The ego-pointed psyche was thus revolutionized and replaced by another goal or magnetic center. Man then strove to characterize this incomprehensible center by innumerable names and symbols such as fish, serpent, monad, cross, paradise, and so on. Meister Eckhart used something of the same symbolism when he tried to characterize Adam's relation to the highest god, on one side, and to the lowest creatures, on the other (par. 294).

I would just like to comment that there could hardly be a better description of the process of individuation. If you think back, for instance, on your own dreams, and their efforts to characterize the unknown center of Self, you can get an idea of how this new formulation and name – that is, the process of individuation – is being assimilated by the matrix of the unconscious, and how similar this assimilation is in *nature* to the assimilation of the figure of the Redeemer, as it is reported by the Gnostics. The language has altered a good deal, it is true; a serpent may now be represented by a train and the spark or ray by the switch to turn on the electric light, but again, just as with the Gnostics, it is as if the unconscious were trying to convey, by all the images in existence, the characteristics of the center to which the one-sided ego must submit.

You will perhaps remember a modern formulation of the same process in *Psychology and Alchemy* but I would just like to remind you of it. At the end of the second part, on dream symbols, Jung is speaking of the symbols of the Self that have appeared in this series of dreams and says that the thing which strikes one most is the consistent development of the central symbol. He says:

> We can hardly escape the feeling that the unconscious process moves spiralwise round a center, gradually getting closer, while the characteristics of the center grow more and more distinct. Or perhaps we could put it the other way round and say that the center – itself virtually unknowable – acts like a magnet on the disparate materials and processes of the unconscious and gradually captures them as in a crystal lattice. For this reason the center is (in other cases) often pictured as a spider in its web, especially when the conscious attitude is still dominated by fear of unconscious processes. But if the process is allowed to take its course, as it was in our

> case, then the central symbol, constantly renewing itself, will steadily and consistently force its way through the apparent chaos of the personal psyche and its dramatic entanglements, just as the great Bernoulli's epitaph says of the spiral: "Eadem mutata resurgo." Accordingly we often find spiral representations of the centre, as for instance the serpent coiled round the creative point, the egg. (Jung 1944, par. 325)

Indeed, it seems as if all the personal entanglements and dramatic changes of fortune that make up the intensity of life were nothing but hesitations, timid shrinkings, almost like petty complications and meticulous excuses for not facing the finality of this strange and uncanny process of crystallization. Often one has the impression that the personal psyche is running round this central point like a shy animal, at once fascinated and frightened, always in flight, and yet steadily drawing nearer. I trust I have given no cause for the misunderstanding that I know anything about the nature of the "center" – for it is simply unknowable and can only be expressed symbolically through its own phenomenology, as is the case, incidentally, with every object of experience.

Looked at psychologically, therefore, the figure of Christ, as a symbol of the Self, acted as a magnetic center to man's unconscious and awoke contents which had been lying dormant and drew them into their right places.

Part 2

Jung begins this part by pointing out how the same process is still at work today. He speaks first of a case of neurosis and of how it is necessary to try to create a wider personality by adding contents from the unconscious, exactly as the unconscious of the early Christian Gnostics, for instance, widened the personality of the old masters to receive the figure of Christ by bringing up the symbols we have been discussing. (The necessity for something of the kind is very visible in the case of St. Paul. He narrowed his outlook more and more into a neurotic cramp against Christ and the Christians through persecution but these boundaries were burst wide open by his vision on the way to Damascus. A lesser man than St. Paul would probably have been broken to pieces by such a sudden vision.) Jung continues by saying that when these contents, which usually appear in dreams or in active imagination, have been assimilated, we find that a new center of gravity gradually emerges, which – though it may thwart the aims of the ego – like a magnet, draws everything into its right place in the original ground plan of the individual. This foundation may already have appeared in the dreams of childhood, for the mandala is there from the beginning, but it can only be understood as a totality, brought into conscious reality, in later life by patient and painstaking work on the contents of the unconscious and on a synthesis between conscious and unconscious (par. 297).

The idea of an unconscious was not unknown to the Gnostics, and Jung brings more than one excerpt that speaks directly of the unconsciousness of the Autopator (father of himself, title of the very first god), though this is not so usual as the idea of the highest god looking down "on the times of ignorance" and being horrified at what the demiurge had created and so getting the work of redemption under way (par. 299). In a footnote, Jung brings the parallel of the krater filled with nous in which the people who yearn for consciousness can obtain nous: "God says that the man filled with Nous should know himself" (par. 299). The Gnostic idea of the deity himself being unconscious is not too unlike the traditional Christian idea that the Old Testament God of Wrath was transformed in the lap of the pure virgin to the New Testament God of Love. Rivkah Schärf-Kluger even showed, in her *Satan in the Old Testament* (1967), that there was a certain transformation and differentiation of the God-image already in the Old Testament. The idea of an unconscious world creator is also found in India (par. 298).

Meister Eckhart's theology also knows of a deity that is not yet lord of itself and which represents an absolute coincidence of opposites. As far as human logic goes, such a state would equal unconsciousness, for where there is no "other," or it has not yet come into being, there is no possibility of increasing consciousness. According to Eckhart, in his original unity the deity knows nothing except the "suprareal" one which he is. Only the father, welling out of the godhead, notices himself, becomes conscious of himself, and the son comes from the father as the first thought of his own being. But as the original godhead is essentially unconscious, so too the man who lives in God. In his sermon on "The Poor in Spirit," Eckhart says:

> The man who has this poverty has everything he was when he lived not in any wise, neither in himself, nor in truth, nor in God. He is so quit and empty of all knowing that no knowledge of God is alive in him; for while he stood in the eternal nature of God, there lived in him not another: what lived there was himself. And so we say this man is as empty of his own knowledge as he was when he was not anything; he lets God work what he will, and he stands empty as when he came from God. (par. 301)

Therefore he should love God in the following way: "Love him as he is: a not-God, a not-spirit, a not-person, a not-image; as a sheer, pure, clear One, which he is, sundered from all secondness; and in this One let us sink eternally, from nothing to nothing" (par. 301).

[I should like to insert a comment here, as this is very easy to misunderstand. As I understand it, Meister Eckhart is saying about the same as the alchemists when, after endless praise of the absolute necessity of reading the books, they suddenly cry: "Tear up the books, that your hearts be not broken," or the Zen masters when they suddenly deride all the knowledge and teaching of the Buddha in order that their pupils may experience instant enlightenment.

It would be very easy to think that Meister Eckhart was extolling original unconsciousness, but, as I understand it, he is recommending a *conscious* return to a state where the opposites are united and not split apart, a *conscious* sacrifice of the ego so that the Self – by definition a pair of united opposites – may be able to work through the human being.]

To return, after this digression, to our chapter: Jung praises Eckhart as the most beautiful flower on the tree of the Free Spirit, which began in the time of Joachim, and says it was no wonder that his writings remained entirely unknown for six hundred years, for only in this century did a public begin to emerge that was capable of appreciating the greatness of his mind (par. 302).

The transformation of the God-image – visible in the quotations – ran parallel to a change in human consciousness; it is impossible to say which is the cause of the other. The God-image is never *invented*, it is experienced, therefore the change may come from the unconscious or may be in the consciousness that apprehends it (par. 303).

The only thing psychology can do is establish the presence of the pictorial images that arise, and it cannot know beforehand what these mean. From the empirical material, these symbols have the character of *wholeness* and therefore presumably mean wholeness. As a rule, they have a unique quality and represent the union of one or two pairs of opposites. They arise from the collision between conscious and unconscious, often when the person feels especially restless or disoriented, and appear as a compensating principle or order. Psychology can only establish that a symbol of wholeness means the wholeness of that individual, but it is also a fact that all the religions have used similar images to express the deity (par. 304).

Jung then mentions many examples and says that empirically such circular and quaternary structures represent the unified wholeness of man. The fact that so many religions call the goal that they represent "God" shows their highly numinous character, and indeed they have an archetypal origin that exceeds every human being's comprehension or power of expression (par. 305).

Part 3

More Gnostic symbols are brought into this part to substantiate the idea of this basic structure of wholeness and of its universal foundation. Jung says that, lest the reader be confused by the vast numbers of Gnostic symbols for the center of our being, he should remember that all this wealth is no more than various aspects of a single transcendental idea of a divine mystery, immanent in all creatures and utterly impossible to describe directly (par. 306).

For the most part, I will leave you to read this rich material for yourselves; I will only mention a very few points.

I would like to include here one description from the ancient Heb Sed festival in Egypt because Jung says all kingships are rooted in this psychology: "The King comes out of an apartment called the sanctuary, then he ascends into a pavilion open at the four sides, with four staircases leading up to it. Carrying the emblems of Osiris, he takes his seat on a throne and turns to the four cardinal points in succession.... It is a kind of second enthronement ... and sometimes the king acts as a priest, making offerings to himself. This last act may be regarded as the climax of the deification of the king" (par. 309).

The king carries the symbol of the Self for every anonymous person in the crowd. All his insignia – crown, mantle, orb, scepter, and so on, show that he represents the cosmic Anthropos, who not only begets but is himself the world. He is the *homo maximus* for whom the Gnostics were always trying to find suitable images and symbols, for they felt that he was the matrix and organizing principle of consciousness. They compared him to an undivided point, the "grain of mustard seed" that grows into the kingdom of heaven. This point is present in the (human) body but this fact is only known to the spiritual and not to the material man. This point which does not exist and consists of nothing becomes an incomprehensible greatness (par. 310).

The Naassenes regarded Naas (serpent) as this central deity and said it was the moist substance, practically water. It pervades everything, like the water of paradise that divides into four. Three of these rivers are regarded as senses: sight, hearing, and smell, but the fourth, the Euphrates, is the mouth which gives out prayer and takes in food. The fourth is always something special, such as the fourth in Daniel's fiery furnace "like a son of God" (par. 311).

After these fragmentary references, I would like to take up the line only at the end of the chapter, because this leads over into the next, which I think we should go into in more detail.

Hippolytus reports that the "universal foundation" for the Naassene Gnostics is the original man, Adam, and that knowledge of him is the bridge to knowledge of God. He is male and female and consists of three parts: the rational, the psychic, and the earthly. These three came down together into one man, Jesus, and the latter is thus related to the original man and is the second Adam. He is the "blessed nature, at once hidden and revealed" of everything that has been and will be; "the kingdom of heaven" which is to be sought within man, even in children of seven years old. For the Naassenes place the "procreative nature in the procreative seed." Jung says, looked at superficially, this begins to look like the beginning of a sexual theory that became so popular in the nineteenth century. But we must not forget that for the Naassenes man's procreative power is only an aspect of the "procreative nature of the whole." This was the hidden and mystical logos for the Naassenes, which they compared to the phallus of Osiris and said, "Osiris is water." The essence of his seed is the cause of all things but does not participate in their nature. Therefore they say: "I become what I will and am what I am," namely, he moves everything but is unmoved himself, and he alone, they say, is good (par. 313).

A further synonym is the ithyphallic Hermes Kyllenios. For they say, "Hermes is the logos, the creator of everything that exists and also of things yet to come in the future." Therefore he is worshipped as the phallus because he – like the male organ – has an urge to rise from below upwards (par. 313).

Part 4

Not only the Logos but Christ himself was drawn into the orbit of sexual symbolism, as we see in a fragment from the *Interrogationes maiores Mariae* quoted by Epiphanius. (This also appears in *Psychology and Alchemy*, but Jung only found it as the latter was going to press, so it is treated at much greater length in *Aion*.) Christ is said to have taken this Mary on to a mountain and to have produced a woman from his side and intercourse with her. The text says: "partaking of his flowing semen, showed that this was to be done, that we might have life" (par. 314).

Jung says that it is very comprehensible that such crude symbolism should not only shock modern susceptibilities but also be rejected by Christians in the third or fourth centuries, and indeed, if it is misunderstood and taken in a purely concrete sense, it can only be rejected. The author shows that he was aware it might cause such a reaction, for Mary got such a shock that she fell to the earth, upon which Christ said to her: "Wherefore do you doubt me, O you of little faith?" This is a reference to John 3:12: "If I have told you earthly things and you do not believe, how can you believe if I tell you heavenly things?" and John 6:54: "Unless you eat the flesh of the Son of man and drink his blood, you have no life in you" (par. 314).

The symbolism is very like what we often find in modern dreams, which also use very concrete images as a sort of "as if" when they seem to be struggling to express an elusive meaning. One gets very used to such language when analyzing dreams, and it is indeed quite possible that the vision in our text arose from some actual visionary experience or dream. It is very clear from the context (John 3:12) that the vision is meant symbolically and not in a concrete sense, for Christ was not speaking of earthly but heavenly things, that is, of a spiritual mystery. It is a mystery, not a secret, for the open language of the vision shows no wish whatever to conceal. It *is* a mystery, however, because consciousness cannot yet apprehend it. We try to analyze dreams, which are also always beyond us, from this angle and will use the same method on this vision.

The *mountain* means ascent, particularly a spiritual ascent to the neighborhood of the spirit and place where God is wont to reveal himself. The *figure of Christ* was, as we have seen, of central importance at that time, and in the realm of Christian Gnosticism he was a manifestation of the Anthropos (original man = Adam). He is the inner man who is reached by Self-knowledge. As Anthropos he is the ordering, quaternary archetype: the squared circle, the Self. Bringing forth the *woman* from his side shows that he was regarded as the second Adam (rib). As Adam is said to have been androgynous before the creation of Eve, so Christ demonstrates his androgynous nature here. The original man is usually hermaphroditic, and we find the symbolism of our vision also in the Vedic tradition. In Christian tradition, this woman would represent the church as the bride of the lamb (par. 319).

The splitting of original man into two means becoming conscious; a tension between the opposites is created which makes consciousness possible. For the Mary who is the spectator of the vision, it would be the projection of an unconscious process in herself. It is the splitting of a unity, presumably of the Anthropos, the incarnate God, and for Mary it would show her that she had only been seeing the pure deified masculinity of Christ and missing the counterbalancing femininity. Therefore, Christ says to her, as it were: "I am both man and woman" (par. 320).

After several medieval references to Christ being androgynous, Jung picks out a vision of Mechthild of Magdeburg's, also on a mountain, where the blessed virgin was awaiting the birth of the divine child. I will not go into the detail of this vision but only mention the significant difference between the two: in the antique vision, the birth of Eve is depicted on the spiritual level of the second Adam. She is, so to speak, a second Eve, a feminine pneuma, the soul as Christ's daughter; whereas Mechthild's vision continues the sacred myth: the daughter-bride brings forth the father in the figure of the son. This son is closely akin to the Self, for we hear that he has a fourfold voice, his heart has four kinds of pulse, and four rays shine from his face. Mechthild's vision is the voice of a new millenium where Eckhart tells us God is born from the soul and where, in Angelus's poems, God and the Self are identical. The times have changed completely, for the procreative power no longer seems to be ascribed to God, but the latter is rather born from the human soul. The mythologem of the young dying god has taken on a psychological form – a sign of further assimilation and realization (par. 321).

To return to Mary's vision: the bringing forth of the woman is followed by sexual union. The *hieros gamos* on a mountain is a well-known motif (Zeus and Hera for instance) and several more incestuous examples are given from alchemy, Egypt, and so on (par. 322).

Our vision has a close connection with some cosmogonic myths, but the theme is not the creation of the world but spiritual renewal. The pouring forth of the semen means a nourishing of life, it happens "that we might have life," as it says. As the text makes clear, the vision is to be understood on the "heavenly" (spiritual) level, so it must be a matter of the *logos spermatikos*, which in the language of the gospels means a living water "springing up into eternal life" (par. 323).

The whole vision is very like some of the symbolism used in alchemy. Its drastic natural language (compared with the reticence of ecclesiastical language) goes back, on the one side, to the expression used in the archaic religions, supposedly overcome long before, and also points forward to a still-crude observation of nature that was just beginning to assimilate the archetype of man. This attempt continued until the seventeenth century (par. 323).

This also perhaps is rather likely to lead to upsets, like the *privatio boni,* but I would not like to pass this story over undiscussed. We come into a field that is very unfamiliar to us in the West, that is, into the realm of impersonal sex.

Alchemy shows us clearly that sex is the force that unites the world opposites, and it seems to me that if only we could reach some understanding of what this is, we should be making a contribution – a grain on humanity's scales – towards the union of the opposites that are held apart by the Iron Curtain today and thereby correspondingly lessening the danger of atomic war. Opposites that are not united must fight according to their nature.

Part 5

After this excursion into the phallic synonyms for the original man, we will go back to the central symbols of the Naassenes and continue with Hermes.

Hermes is a conjurer of spirits, a guide of souls and a begetter of souls. He "brought down the souls from the Blessed Man on high…into the form of clay, that they may serve the Demiurge of this creation, Esaldaios, a fiery god, the fourth by number." This refers to the fourth person, the devil, who is opposed to the Trinity (par. 325).

Hermes has the golden wand, with which he "drops sleep into the eyes of the dead and wakes up the sleepers." The Naassenes were referring to Ephesians 5:14: "Awake, O sleeper, and arise from the dead, and Christ shall give you light" (par. 326).

There is a close parallel between the lapis of the alchemists and that of the Naassenes, who use the symbol of the rock or stone for their inner man, both taking it from the well-known allegory of Christ as the corner stone. Both say that their stone or inner man was "cut from the mountain without hands," and Epiphanius tells us that the mountain is the arch man Christ, from whom the stone or inner man was cut (par. 326).

The Anthropos is the logos whom the souls follow "twittering," as the bats follow Hermes in the *nekyia*. They follow him to Oceanus, the origin of god and man. Men are born from ebb tide and gods from the flow. That, they say, is what is meant by the words "I have said, you are gods and all of you the sons of the most High." The relationship or even identity of God and man is clearly stated, in the Bible no less than in the Naassene doctrines (par. 327).

This is again a point that is very easy to misunderstand. As Jung points out, Christ himself – and it is included in the orthodox Bible – says: "Ye are gods." Now this is usually either passed over or identified with when it leads to a monumental inflation. The asylums are full of men who believe they are Christ.

Perhaps the clearest simile Jung uses is when he says that the human being must never forget he is only the stable in which the god is born. Yet we seem to have some choice as to whether we will function as that stable or not. Here we really come to the crux of the process of individuation: are we willing to sacrifice the ego as a self-willed one-sided limited human consciousness and are we willing to realize the eternal Self and live its pattern instead of our own? That – as well as I can express it – is the psychological meaning of Christ's statement "Ye are gods," but perhaps it is easier to understand in St. Paul's: "I live, yet not I, Christ liveth in me" (Gal. 2:20).

Part 6

In this part, we begin with the *quaternios* that play a much greater role in chapter 14. The Naassenes derived all things from a triad: the natures of the blessed man on high, the lower man, and the "kingless race begotten from above." But four figures are mentioned as belonging to this third race (one might call it the middle between high and low): Miriam, the searched for one; Jethro the great wise one; Sephora (Zipporah, Moses' wife), the seer; and Moses, whose descendants did not stay in Egypt. Jung then goes into the marriage *quaternios* as shown by the Gnostics, but as this comes in much more detail in the next chapter, we will postpone it until then (par. 328).

Jung then goes into the other names for the Naassene triad. The only thing I wish to mention here is that it is again the third that is picked out as the "upwards flowing Jordan," the flow (begetter of the gods, as we saw before), and this Jordan is also the human hermaphrodite in all things, whom the ignorant call Geryon of the threefold body, but the Greeks call the "celestial horn of the moon." The text also mentions the quaternity, just spoken of, as the equivalent of these and also of the logos (par. 330).

The logos or quaternity is also the cup of Anacreon (from which the king drew his omens), and Hippolytus goes on to the miracle at Cana and points out that the wine was the kingdom of heaven, for it lies in us as wine in a cup. This cup again is parallel to the ithyphallic gods who signify the original man and the reborn spiritual man, who is "in every respect consubstantial" with the original man, which is why Christ said we must eat his body and drink his blood for, says Hippolytus, Christ "was conscious of the *individual nature* of each of his disciples," and also of the *necessity for each "to come to his own special nature"* (par. 331).

[I must insert a comment here, for it strikes me that this very psychological formulation is amazing in a second-century text. It has the whole of the universal and individual, even unique nature of the Self (Atman and Purusha) in that *all* must eat and drink (in a substantial sense) the body and blood of the archetypal universal Christ, but in order that they may become their own special individual selves.]

Aion goes on with some more orthodox Christian parallels to the partly pagan ideas of the Gnostics, in order to give the reader a more complete picture of the spirit of the first two centuries of our era. Jung shows the difficulties that the Christians get into by translating the Greek word *teleios* as "perfect" instead of "whole." Even St. Paul got into this trap when he declares in the third chapter of Philippians that he is *not* yet perfect and three verses later says: "Let us then, as many as are perfect, be of this mind," and in other texts we hear that the "perfect man" is nevertheless in need of renewal through rebirth (par. 333).

The father of this "perfectus," according to Hippolytus, is the higher man, the Anthropos. He is a bringer of peace and quells the war of the elements in the human body, a statement we also meet in alchemy of its *filius philosophorum*. He is also called a corpse because he is buried in the body like the mummy in a tomb. We find the same idea in Paracelsus where the "mumia" corresponds exactly to the original man (par. 334).

The dead man, says Hippolytus, will rise again by passing through the "door of heaven," which Jacob saw in his famous dream on the way to Mesopotamia, which country again is the "stream of the great ocean that flows from the midst of the perfect man." Many other quotations are given referring to this life-giving water. Christ himself is this water and flows into the world through the four gospels, like the four rivers of paradise (par. 336).

These quotations (to which I have done no justice whatever but which you will have read for yourselves) show how many connections there are between the Gnostic and ecclesiastical sources. Gnostic symbolism uses the language of the church again and again, and the church fathers, particularly Origen, constantly amplify very much in the same way as the Gnostics.

Part 7

Coming back to the Gnostic symbols listed by Hippolytus: the original man in his latent state is called *Aipolos*, because he is the pole that turns the cosmos round, a parallel to what the alchemists say of Mercurius. The Naassenes also call Aipolos *Proteus*, whom they say always tells the truth. (Jung then tells the well-known story from the Odyssey, where Proteus will change into many shapes but must be forced back into his original shape before he will answer questions.) (par. 338)

Proteus is also likened to the green ear of corn in the Eleusinian mysteries. The cry "Brimo has born Brimos" is addressed to him. A lower correspondence is the dark path of Persephone but men need this lower path, "the sickness of love," in order to be initiated into the "great and celestial mysteries." In a footnote, this is compared to the southern Indian temple, visited in 1937 by Jung, which is covered in obscene sculptures in order to remind ordinary people of sexuality, for if they tried to follow the spiritual path directly, Yama, the god of death, could instantly carry them off. Only the man who has lived out his karma in this respect, in this or earlier existences, is destined to tread the spiritual path. So two seductresses are portrayed at the gate of the temple and the lingam (phallus) is in the innermost holy of holies. All this was explained to Jung in the temple by a Tantrist pundit (par. 339).

Part 8

The last section is concerned with the indivisible point, the monad.

Monoïmos speaks of Oceanus, the origin of gods and men, as a single monad, uncompounded and indivisible, yet compounded and divisible, loving and at peace with all things and yet at war with all things, unlike and like itself, as it were, a musical harmony containing everything. The symbol of the complete man is a jot or tittle. This single indivisible jot (monad) is yet many-faced, thousand-eyed and named, the jot of the iota. The son of man is the one point, containing everything in himself. (The above is very much shortened.) (par. 340)

Jung remarks that this paradoxical idea of the monad is a description of the Self, by a thinker of the second century A.D. (par. 341). An interesting parallel from Plotinus, in the third century A.D., then follows, but I will leave you to read this for yourselves. (The point in the circle as an image of God is mentioned very often, as you know, in Jung's books.) The idea of the spark (*scintilla*), which we know well from alchemy and Meister Eckhart, is then documented from various Gnostic doctrines and the idea of the point is gone into in alchemy where it has almost exactly the same meaning as in Gnosticism (par. 344).

The chapter ends by pointing out that we can see from all these suggestions how Christ was assimilated through symbols that also are valid for the kingdom of heaven. Christ and his kingdom have the same meaning. This fact has been criticized as a dissolution of Christ's personality, but this criticism ignores the fact that it also represents an assimilation and integration of Christ in the human soul. The result is to be seen in the production of human personality and the development of consciousness. It is true that these specific gains are most seriously threatened now in the anti-Christian age, and not only by the delusions of the totalitarian states, but above all and primarily by the rationalistic hubris that is tearing consciousness away from its transcendental roots and holding ego-conceived goals before its eyes (par. 346).

XIV

The Structure and Dynamics of the Self

PART 1

The examples given in the last chapter illustrate the gradual assimilation and amplification by ego consciousness of the archetype that lies beneath it. Rather than add to their number, Jung attempts a summary in this chapter, to give as general a picture as possible.

Hippolytus makes it clear that the Gnostics were really psychologists. They speak, for instance, of the great difficulty in finding and comprehending the soul and of knowing the whole man. Clement of Alexandria says, for example: "Therefore, as it seems, it is the greatest of all disciplines to know oneself; for when a man knows himself, he knows God." Monoïmos gives direct psychological advice when he writes to Theophrastus of how to find God in oneself by examining who or what it is that makes one do the very things one does not intend (par. 347).

One finds exactly the same idea in the Upanishads in such sentences as: "Who sends forth the speech we utter here? What god is it that stirs the eye and ear?" And even: "He is your Self, the inner controller, the immortal" (par. 348).

Monoïmos *might* have been influenced by Indian thought for he is called "the Arab," but his statements are very important because they show that, even in the second century A.D., the ego was thought of as the exponent of an all-embracing totality, a thought that by no means all psychologists have got around to today. These insights show an intense introspective observation and reveal that the Gnosis is undoubtedly psychological knowledge and that its contents come from the unconscious. They reached their knowledge by concentrating their attention on the so-called "subjective factor," which consists empirically in the demonstrable influence that the collective unconscious has on consciousness, which explains the amazing parallels found in Gnostic symbolism and the present-day products of the psychology of the unconscious (par. 350).

Before illustrating this parallelism, Jung briefly reviews the facts that led psychology to assume an archetype of wholeness: dreams and visions and active imagination, both of which contained innumerable symbols of totality. Then he goes into a detailed description of mandalas, based on the circle and square, which lead him on to geometrically formed crystals and the miraculous stone. Analogies lead from here to the city, castle, church, house, room, and vessel, all of which are symbols that emphasize the fact that the ego is contained in the far greater Self, and further the symbol of the wheel, which points to ritual circumambulation. The symbol of the wheel concentrates the attention on the center (from which the wheel rolls) and can be formulated by a point. This symbol is related to the heavenly pole and the starry bowl of the sky rotating round it and to the horoscope as the "wheel of birth" (par. 351).

The images of the house and vessel bring us to the inhabitant and liquid (water) contained in each. Apart from geometrical and arithmetical symbols, a human figure is the commonest symbol of the Self in modern material. Just as the circle is contrasted with the square, so positive human figures (gods, godlike human beings, great men or women, positive parents, and so on) are contrasted with negative figures (demons, devouring parents, and the like), for the Self, like all archetypes, consists of paradoxes and antinomies. Although indeed it is quite possible that the seeming paradox is only a reflection of the enantiodromian changes of the conscious attitude which – it seems – can have a favorable or unfavorable effect on the whole. Our attitude to it does affect the unconscious in general, and it is wise to consider contradictory manifestations of the unconscious in connection with our conscious attitude. We should underrate neither conscious nor unconscious, because – apart from what the conscious may call forth – there are too many proofs of the autonomous character of the unconscious for us to be able to seek the origin of antinomies entirely in the conscious mind. One affects the other and there is a kind of "uncertainty relationship" between them (par. 353).

The Self can appear in every shape and form, from the highest to the lowest, and naturally also has its theriomorphic symbolism. The most frequent of its animal images in modern dreams in Jung's experience are elephants, horses, bulls, bears, black and white birds, fish, or serpents, although tortoises, snails, spiders, and beetles also sometimes appear. The principal plant symbols are flowers and trees and, among inorganic symbols, the mountain and lake probably occur most frequently (par. 356).

When sexuality has been undervalued, the Self usually appears in the symbol of the phallus. The undervaluation can consist in ordinary repression or in an obvious depreciation. The latter – in certain differentiated people – is caused by a purely biological interpretation and evaluation of sexuality which entirely overlooks the spiritual (or mystical) implications of the sexual instinct. Yet the latter have existed as psychic facts from time immemorial, though these facts are ever and again devalued and repressed for rational or philosophical reasons. In all such cases, one can expect an unconscious phallicism by way of compensation. A good example is to be found in Freud, whose main approach – as is well known – to the psyche was from the sexual angle (par. 357).

Part 2

Jung points out that the Naassenes, as described by Hippolytus, laid the most emphasis on human images, and he returns to the symbol mentioned briefly in the last chapter, which Jung calls the Moses *quaternio* for short, and in the second place to the paradise *quaternio* with the four rivers of paradise. These two will not only be related to each other, but also to the later alchemistic quaternities,[6] or it can also be represented in layers when it looks like this:

Positive Jethro	———	Miriam as positive anima
Moses as culture hero	———	Zipporah as higher mother
Lower Adam as ordinary man	———	Eve as ordinary woman
Moses as carnal man	———	The Ethiopian woman
Jethro as heathen priest	———	Miriam, negative as leper

Now the emphasized Gnostic quaternity, as we see in the diagram (*Aion*, p. 227), only includes the upper three layers where it is in a sense unsymetrical and leads only upwards and thus to a *senarius* (six). But the figures are so skillfully chosen that the incest motif (so emphasized in alchemy) is not missing and the two lower (shadow) layers are hinted at in the biblical facts that Moses married the Ethiopian (a black woman) and that Miriam was so furious that she became leprous (negative), and although Jethro is *not* represented negatively in the Bible, yet he was a Midianite priest and did not serve Yahweh and leaves the "chosen people" to go to his own home. He was very wise and most helpful to Moses and is thus characterized as a numinous personality, an archetypal image, which, as we see again and again, is always dual natured, positive and negative. So Moses, as culture hero, represents the light positive side of his personality and, as the husband of the dark woman, his own carnal shadow, and Jethro, as the wise old man, also represents his own shadow as a stranger and pagan priest, presumably with magical and nefarious qualities (par. 358).

This Gnostic *quaternio* is a variation of the almost universal cross-cousin marriage *quaternio* that is always characterized by an incest nuance (par. 361; see also Jung 1946, par. 410–449).

Jung then combines the layers, mentioned before, in a more elaborate diagram.[7] (It is unfortunate that in the more elaborate English edition, the word "Man" does not stand clearly and simply between the upper and lower quaternities, exposed to the full tension, as he does in the German. The printing of "The Anthropos Quaternio" and the "Shadow Quaternio," names that appear in the text but not in the diagram in the German, has complicated it.) The lowest point in this diagram is not the lower Adam but the serpent, who in Genesis was created before man and was the Naas that gave these Gnostics their name: the Naassenes.

Jung then goes into the dark aspect of the metaphysical figures in Gnosticism, which gave such offense to the orthodox fathers of the church, and points out that though the serpent has its positive side (wisdom), it has also always had its negative aspect, for instance, as the Apophis serpent in Egypt (which tries to swallow the boat of the sun god Ra every night) and as the devil, "the ancient serpent," in Christianity. He then gives a lot of interesting material which I will leave you to read for yourselves (par. 366).

Part 3

It is very meaningful that Gnostic philosophy was continued in alchemy. Mater Alchimia is one of the mothers of modern science, which later has given us such unparalleled knowledge of the "dark side" of matter, making the very roots of human existence the theme of its research. The human mind has thus sunk deep into the sublunary world of matter and has thus repeated the Gnostic myth of Nous, who – seeing his reflection in the depths below – plunged down and was swallowed in the embrace of the physis (just as we are – if we really face the fact – today). Jung traces this development and points out that the wheel of history has turned back two thousand years and has produced an entirely pre-Christian revival of despotism, a lack of individual rights, of cruelty, indignity, and slavery where the labor problem is solved by the Ergastulum (slave or concentration camp). The moral reversal of all values is thus being enacted before our very eyes (par. 368).

This development seems to have been anticipated in medieval and Gnostic symbolism, just as the Antichrist was in the New Testament. This came to pass because the higher Adam corresponded to the lower, and these old thinkers – though consciously they strove upwards towards the spirit in the Anthropos quaternity – never forgot man's instinctual disposition which has its roots in the animal kingdom (that is, the shadow quaternity). The lowest point of this kingdom is the cold-blooded snake which – contrary to all expectations – turns out to be the counterpart of the Anthropos. It was indeed already a well-known allegory of Christ, well equipped with the gifts of wisdom and spirituality (par. 369).

The fact that the shadow *quaternio* has its roots in the animal kingdom is found very early. Origen already said: "So when thou seest that thou hast all the things the world has, doubt not that thou hast within thee even the animals which are offered in sacrifice." But as the shadow is unconscious in most people, its nadir, the serpent, where the possibility of relationship ceases, naturally represents the deepest unconsciousness (par. 370).

The inferior personality, the shadow, can no longer be differentiated in its lowest layer from the instinctivity of the animal, which possesses its own peculiar wisdom and sometimes a knowledge that seems supernatural to us. This is the "treasure" that the serpent or dragon guards and the reason that, on the one side, it is wisdom per se and a cold, ruthless, dangerous unrelatedness on the other (par. 370).

In alchemy the serpent is the symbol of *Mercurius non vulgi*, who was bracketed with Hermes, the god of revelation. Both are pneumatic in nature, though Mercurius is a chthonic spirit that dwells in matter and represents a piece of the original chaos, of the *massa confusa* (par. 371).

The paradise *quaternio* runs parallel to the Moses *quaternio* in the Naassene Gnostics, and here the serpent is a personified tree numen and is usually traditionally depicted in the tree. It is the voice of the tree that convinced Eve – in Luther's version – that: "It would be good to eat of the tree and pleasant to behold that it is a lusty tree" (par. 372).

Paradise was also a favorite symbol of the *albedo* in alchemy, the regained state of innocence, and the source of its four rivers is a symbol for their *aqua permanens*. Christ is this source for the church fathers, and paradise is the foundation of the soul from which the fourfold river of the logos arises (par. 373).

Part 4

The serpent has led us back to the images of paradise, tree and earth, which is an evolutionary regression from the animal kingdom back to the plants and inorganic matter, whose mysterious secret is symbolized by the lapis in alchemy. In this connection, indeed, it is more the initial material, for the lapis is both the beginning and end product of alchemy (par. 374).

Jung then gives another double pyramid diagram with the four rivers of paradise in place of the four figures, the serpent above and the lapis below.[8] He points out that the lapis is not just an allegory of Christ but a direct parallel, that is, the Anthropos, so that the nadir of this paradise *quaternio* is again a counterpart of the Anthropos (par. 375).

Yet another double pyramid diagram – called in the English version the "Lapis Quaternio" – follows, in which the four rivers of paradise (or four figures) are replaced by the four elements: the serpent above by the lapis and the lapis below by the rotundum.[9] In the initial stage of the lapis, the elements are not united; on the contrary they are hostile to each other, and the task of the alchemistic opus is to restore the unity of the lapis in the realm of the inorganic and redeem it from its split-up condition. Paracelsus and his followers called this initial condition of the *prima materia* "the increatum" and regarded it as co-eternal with God, rightly comparing it to the earth in Genesis, which was "without form and void, and darkness was upon the face of the deep and the spirit of God moved upon the face of the deep" (Gen. 1:2). The primary substance is round like the world and the world soul. According to the old view, the soul is round and the vessel, in which the transformation takes place, must be round too. Dorn says that the vessel "should be made from a kind of squaring of the circle, so that the spirit and soul of our material, separated from its body, may raise the body with them to the height of their own heaven." The anonymous author of the scholia to the *Tractatus Aureus* says: "Reduce your stone to the four elements, rectify and combine them into one and you will have the whole magistery. This One, to which the elements must be reduced, is that little circle in the centre of this squared figure. It is the mediator making peace between the enemies or elements." Later he depicts this vessel as the philosophical Pelican (par. 376).

Dorn comments: "A is the inside, as it were the origin and source from which the other letters flow, and likewise the final goal to which all the others flow back, as rivers flow into the ocean" (par. 378).[10] Jung says that this explanation suffices to show us that the vessel is a mandala that symbolizes the Self, like the higher Adam and his four emanations and Horus and his four sons. Therefore Maria Prophetissa says: "The Philosophers teach everything except the Hermetic vessel, because that is divine and hidden from the Gentiles by the Lord's wisdom" (par. 378).

These quotations – and many more that I have omitted – show us that the vessel had a most unusual and great significance. Naturally this can only be understood "philosophically," that is, psychologically, when it would mean: "Make the hermetic vessel out of your psychic wholeness" and pour the *aqua permanens* or *aqua doctrinae* into it, which would suggest that the adept should "inwardly digest" and transform himself through the alchemistic doctrine (par. 379).

Jung ends this part by saying that the round hermetic vessel in which the mysterious transformation takes place has the significance of the Deity, the (platonic) world soul and the wholeness of man. So again it is a counterpart of the Anthropos and, at the same time, of the universe in its smallest and most material form. This makes it easy to understand why the first attempts to construct a model of the atom took the planetary system as a pattern (par. 380).

I would like to comment briefly on Jung saying that the alchemistic vessel – understood psychologically – would mean our own wholeness into which we must pour the *aqua permanens* or *vinum ardens*. Practically this would amount to finding our own limits – for each person has his or her own degree of wholeness – and then pouring psychological knowledge into this vessel of our own individual wholeness.

Every basic analysis begins with the hypothesis of the analysand's wholeness. This hypothesis is justified again and again, so that the analyst learns that he can trust it. Each dream is a fact, an expression of this wholeness, and slowly one pours in the *aqua* of self-knowledge. The end result or goal is the *vas* of individual wholeness being filled with living *consciousness*. The *vinum ardens* could be called intensified spiritual life. The more unconscious people are, the more dull and boring their effect, but the nearer to individuation they come, the more exciting and winelike their effect. One saw that marvelously with Jung. Just to be near him was life-giving and practically everybody who knew him recognized that fact.

It really follows the idea of the logion – which Jung himself quoted so often: "Man, if indeed thou knowest what thou doest, thou art blessed; but if thou knowest not, thou art cursed, and a transgressor of the law" (James 1924, p. 33; see also Jung 1938, par. 394).

Part 5

This part begins with the reasons why the quaternity is an organizing scheme *par excellence*, resembling the crossed threads used in a telescope. The number four is instinctively used to divide the earth (points of the compass), course of the year (seasons), and so on. Therefore it is not at all surprising that the Gnostics used a quaternity, more or less consciously, to establish some order in the chaotic and numerous images that poured in on them from the unconscious (par. 381).

They use the pattern of the primitive cross-cousin marriage but the purely biological character of this has given way to a more cultural level, that is, the loss of the cousin attribute has been compensated – as is usually the case – by magical qualities or exalted rank. In psychological language: a projection of anima and animus has taken place which constellates the unconscious in the marriage relationship, that is, the marriage has become psychologically complicated. It is no longer a purely biological and social coexistence and is beginning to become a conscious relationship (par. 381).

The Gnostics also used, as we have seen, the quaternity of the rivers of paradise to organize their apparently disconnected symbols. Both these quaternities are near parallels to the series of pictures that are still produced in active imagination and in chaotic psychic states. They are a compensation and ordering factor in the confusion caused by an invasion of unconscious contents, and these require an ordering principle, exactly like the contents of Gnosticism and alchemy (par. 382).

As it is advisable to proceed historically, Jung says that he used the Moses *quaternio* of the Naassenes as a starting point, because this is directly founded on the primitive cross-cousin pattern, but it could be based on any other marriage *quaternio*, but not on Horus and his four sons, for instance, because the feminine is missing and therefore does not represent the extreme opposites (par. 383).

Jung then returns to the two *quaternios*.[11] The Anthropos *quaternio* corresponds to the Gnostic model, but the second (shadow *quaternio*) is constructed from the biblical text. The higher *quaternio* must have a shadow, because man (the lower Adam) possesses an undeniable chthonic psyche and therefore cannot be expressed only by a *quaternio* that is superior to him (par. 384).

Now just as the Anthropos finds his symmetrical complement in the lower Adam, so the lower Adam (man) finds his symmetrical complement in the serpent. The choice of this symbol is not only based on their mutual relation in Eden, but also because the serpent is the most usual symbol for the dark chthonic world of instinct. And it is also a symbol of wisdom and could outwit Adam from the beginning. The serpent seems to have been equipped by God with a superhuman intelligence (par. 385).

So man culminates above in the idea of a light, good God and rests below on a dark principle, the serpent that personifies Adam's disobedience. And the serpent again has its complement in the second Naassene quaternity. Paradise takes us into the world of plants and animals, a garden enlivened by animals and the acme of all growing things. As *serpens mercurialis*, the serpent is not only related to Hermes, the god of revelation but, as a vegetation numen, calls forth the "blessed greenness." This serpent dwells even in the interior of the earth and is the spirit hidden in the stone (par. 386).

The symmetrical complement of the serpent then is the stone as representative of the earth, and here we enter a later development of the symbolism, the alchemistic lapis. Just as the serpent forms the lower opposite of man, so the lapis complements the serpent. But it again corresponds to man, for it is not only often represented in human form but has a "body, soul and spirit," is a homunculus and a symbol of the Self. It is not, however, a human ego but more a collective soul, like the Indian *hiranyagarbha*, a golden seed. The lapis is the father and mother of all metals, a hermaphrodite (par. 387).

The choice of this symbol also is not arbitrary, we find it in alchemistic literature from the first to the eighteenth century. Although it is an "ultimate unity," it is yet produced by the splitting and putting together of the four elements from the rotundum. The rotundum is a highly abstract, transcendental idea that by reason of its wholeness and roundness refers to the Anthropos (par. 388).

Thus our four double pyramids arrange themselves in a circle and would form the well-known Ouroboros. The rotundum as the fifth stage would then be identical with the first, that is, the heavy darkness of the earth, metal, has a secret relationship to the Anthropos. This is very evident in alchemy, but we also meet it in the history of religion where the metals grow from Gayomart's blood. This curious relationship is explained by the identity of lowest and highest, as we have already seen in the serpent that is a chthonic and yet a "most spiritual animal." The rotundum is the world soul and a "blessed God" for Plato (par. 389).

Part 6

Jung says he will condense the ideas in the last chapter and represent them graphically.[12]

The point of greatest tension between the opposites is represented by the serpent, which is an allegory of Christ as well as the devil and so contains and symbolizes the strongest polarity into which the Anthropos falls when he descends into the physis. The ordinary man has not reached this point of tension, but it is in his unconscious, that is, in the serpent (par. 390).

In a footnote, Jung points out that most people have not a sufficiently wide range of consciousness to become aware of the opposites in human nature. The tension then remains unconscious but can and does appear in dreams. But release of an unconscious force is a danger, and the more unconscious this is, the more dangerous it will be. Therefore, the wider the split between conscious and unconscious becomes, the greater the danger of psychic infection and mass psychosis. The loss of our symbols has broken down our bridge to the unconscious; and instinct then no longer warns us against unsound ideas and empty slogans. If rationality is not rooted in tradition and instinct, it cannot save us from any absurdity (par. 390).

To return to the main text: the opposites are united in the lapis, the counterpart of man, but with a visible join, the symbol of the hermaphrodite. In the higher Adam and rotundum the opposition is invisible, but presumably they stand in opposition to each other.

The arrangement in the Ouroboros shows a stronger tension between the Anthropos, rotundum, and the serpent than between the homo and lapis, which is shown in the distance.[13] The arrows indicate the descent into the physis and ascent towards the spiritual. The fact that all these symbols are antinomies is in keeping with the paradoxical nature of alchemy (par. 391).

[I should like to point out that it would also be possible to arrange all our four diagrams in a circle, as the Ouroboros, because each one has a common symbol with the next. Man is the lowest image of the Anthropos quaternity and the highest of the shadow quaternity. The serpent is the lowest of the shadow quaternity and the highest of the paradise quaternity. The lapis is the lowest of the paradise quaternity and the highest of the lapis quaternity. When we come to the beginning and the end – the top of the Anthropos quaternity and the bottom of the lapis quaternity – we get the usual dual character of the fourth, in that it is both rotundum and Anthropos, but obviously they are both symbols for one and the same thing: the Self.]

A picture of the four elements from a book of Michael Maier is then considered in detail, but as it is very complicated and also not absolutely indispensable for the main line, I will leave you to study it for yourselves and return to the text where Jung says that one of the factors in a quaternity has an exceptional position, which can also be expressed by its duplex nature. The Euphrates (the fourth of the paradise rivers), for instance, signifies the mouth where the food goes in and also where prayers go out. In the Moses *quaternio*, Moses' wife plays the double role of Zipporah and the Ethiopian woman, and in alchemy Mercurius is male and female. This characteristic can also be seen in the space-time *quaternio*, where there are three dimensions of space and the fourth can be conceived as time. But time again has three qualities (past, present, and future), and then static space, in which changes of state take place, must be added as the fourth. In both cases the fourth represents an incommensurable other that is needed for their mutual determination. The other, the fourth, appears in all the quaternities that we have been considering, and the fourth in the Christian Trinity, if one may use such an expression, would be Mary or the devil (par. 397).

The space-time *quaternio* is the archetypal condition and the opportunity to apprehend the physical world at all. It corresponds in structure to the psychological four functions. (The fourth inferior function has also this double character, in that the ego is unable to use it on account of its weak and inferior quality and yet, used by the Self, it brings us our most valuable gifts (par. 398).

Jung then refers the reader to a mandala reproduced in his paper on mandalas (Jung 1950b, p. 309) and then speaks of a picture in a manuscript by Joachim of Flora (Jung 1951, p. 254a) and of a peculiar theory of world creation in the Clementine Homilies, but I will leave you to study these for yourselves.

At the end of this chapter Jung looks back over the course our argument has taken. The two Naassene quaternities, the positive Moses and paradise, stood at the beginning. One is above man and the other apparently below him. But whereas the Gnostics place man in close connection with the upper (Moses) quaternity, they separate him from the chthonic animal and plant world of paradise. This is characteristic for the age of Gnosticism and early Christianity; man only looked upwards. But we cannot rise higher and higher, such a movement inevitably ends below. Therefore we now feel impelled to symmetrize the lower Adam with a shadow quaternity, corresponding to the upper Anthropos quaternity. This was not necessary in the days of the Gnostics, the trend then was upwards, but we can no longer conceive of a psyche that is oriented only upwards and know that it must be balanced by an equally strong consciousness of our lower man. This is specifically a modern state of affairs and puts man in the center of a field of consciousness where he has never before stood consciously. Earlier he could only see Christ as the mediator between God and the world but through his meditation on this image, he in a way gradually took over the mediating role. The image of Christ – crucified between the two thieves, one of whom went up and other down – gradually woke man up to his shadow and its dual nature, which had already been anticipated by the double meaning of the serpent. Just as the serpent stands for healing and destruction, and the thieves for two diametrically different destinies, so the shadow is, on the one side, regrettable and reprehensible weakness and, on the other, healthy instinctiveness, the prerequisite for higher consciousness (par. 402).

The shadow quaternity to balance man's middle position only becomes necessary when man begins to be more aware of his own existence and the need to become more conscious of himself has become stronger than his dependence on the deity. We complete the picture by the shadow quaternity, because this corresponds to the historical development. The early complete dependence on the higher pneumatic sphere, where man just clung like a child to its mother, was threatened by the kingdom of Satan, and man's early dependence on deliverance from this threat by a redeemer, who could conquer everything for him, was strongly reinforced by his belief in an immediate second coming of Christ. But when this great hope was dashed and man was left with disappointed great expectations, a certain regression became inevitable and the libido necessarily flowed back to man and heightened his consciousness of himself. This slowly led to separation from the upper pneumatic sphere and an approach to the realm of the shadow. This increased man's moral consciousness and his feeling of being redeemed became relative. The church found herself obliged to lay greater stress on the significance and power of *her ritual* in order to put up a barrier against the inrush of the world, but she thus inevitably became a "kingdom of this world." The transition to the shadow quaternity illustrates the historical development of the second millenium A.D. (par. 403).

PART 7

We come to the seventh and last part of the fourteenth chapter, where the movement and dynamics of the Self become very evident. This part requires reading very carefully and repeatedly and is very difficult to summarize. I shall only attempt a very brief and most inadequate outline.

A stands for the initial state (the Anthropos, in this case) and for the end state.[14] *B*, *C*, and *D* stand for the intermediate states. *We must not forget that it is a matter of the continual transformation of one and the same substance*. *A* will produce *a*, *B* will produce *b*, and, as this is a psychological formula, we may also assume that *a* is followed by *b* and that the formula runs from left to right, that is, that the transformation turns rightwards with the sun, a process of becoming conscious. Modern scientific thinking is based on a trinity of principles (space, time, and causality), but here we are not moving in modern scientific thought but in the classical and medieval point of view which, up to the time of Leibnitz, recognized the principle of correspondence that Jung calls synchronicity as a fourth. Our Gnostic quaternity is a naive product of the unconscious and therefore represents a psychic fact that can be related to the four functions of consciousness (par. 410).

The formula reproduces the essential features of the symbolic process of transformation. It shows the rotation of the mandala, the antithetical play of the complementary (or compensatory) processes and then the apocatastasis, that is, the restoration of an original state of wholeness. But it can only hint at the higher plane that is reached through the process of transformation and integration. The progress consists of an unfolding of the totality into four parts, four entities, which means they have been subjected to discrimination by the four functions which alone changes the originally unconscious totality into a *conscious* one (par. 410).

[This explains the conviction, which one meets again and again in analysis, that nothing has been achieved, that one is back in the same old place. One has to return, to meet it with another function, so to speak, but this return is a part of the process of transformation, and not at all necessarily a regression.]

We can also express it as the Anthropos. *A* descending from above, through his shadow *B*, into the physis *C* (serpent), and then – through a kind of crystallization process *D* (= lapis) that reduces chaos to order – the Anthropos rises again to his original state which has now been transformed from an unconscious to a conscious condition (par. 410).

I should like to return to a passage which I already quoted in the introduction, because it is much clearer here in its context.

> The formula presents a symbol of the self, for the self is not just a static quantity or constant form, but is also a dynamic process. In the same way, the ancients saw the *imago Dei* in man not as a mere imprint, as a sort of lifeless, stereotyped impression, but as an active force. The four transformations represent a process of restoration or rejuvenation taking place, as it were, inside the self, and comparable to the carbon-nitrogen cycle in the sun, where a carbon nucleus captures four protons (two of which immediately become neutrons) and releases them at the end of the cycle in the form of an alpha particle. The carbon nucleus itself comes out of the reaction unchanged, "like the Phoenix from the ashes." The secret of existence, i.e., the existence of the atom and its components, may well consist in a continually repeated process of rejuvenation, and one comes to similar conclusions in trying to account for the numinosity of the archetypes. (par. 411)

Jung points out that he is fully aware of the extremely hypothetical nature of the comparison, but he thinks it worth risking a mistake, for sooner or later nuclear physics and psychology must draw closer together as they push forward from different directions into transcendental territory, the one with the concept of the atom, and the other with that of the archetype (par. 412).

Psyche cannot be wholly different from matter or how could it move matter? And how could matter produce psyche? They exist in one and the same world and each must partake of the other (par. 413).

Since analogy formation is a law that largely governs the life of the psyche, we may expect that our apparently purely speculative construction is no new invention but will also be found in earlier thought. Jung then speaks briefly of such a schema in the *Book of Pseudo Platonic Tetralogies*, which he dealt with at much greater length in *Psychology and Alchemy* (1944). I will leave you to look it up there for yourselves.

Jung then speaks of the age-old Ars Geomantica or the art of punctuation, which has a similar formation. You will find considerably more about this in the article on "Synchronicity" (Jung 1952b).

Then a quaternary system of Athanasius Kircher is spoken of, which I want to quote only the last sentence: "You can see from these unities how the perceiving senses go back to reason, and reason to intelligence, and intelligence to God, where in a perfect cycle is found the beginning and the consummation" (par. 417).

After another example from Michael Maier, Jung mentions that the same idea of the circular opus can be found in Chinese alchemy and quotes from the text of *The Golden Flower*: "When the light is allowed to move in a circle, all the powers of Heaven and Earth, of the Light and the Dark, are crystallised" (par. 418).

The circular apparatus to assist this circular process appears as early as Olympiodorus (second century A.D.), and Dorn thinks that this "circular movement of the Physiochemists" comes from the earth, the lowest element. We also find the basic idea of the ascent and descent in the Tabula Smaragdina, and the stages of the transformation are depicted again and again in the alchemistic texts, for instance, in the Ripley Scroll.[15] All these should be regarded as indirect attempts to depict the still-unconscious "process of individuation."

[I would just like to comment here, as I warned you at the beginning, that if I have used the term *process of individuation* rather sparingly, this has been because the process was still unconscious in almost all our examples. Nevertheless, practically everything we have been considering has always had the same foundation: what we now call the process of individuation.]

XV

Conclusion

We have come to the end of our long, difficult, and – to me at all events – very rewarding book.

In the conclusion, Jung once again sums up his aim in writing this book, which is above all to elucidate and amplify the most important of all the archetypes for modern man to understand: the archetype of the Self or, in other words, the process of individuation (par. 422).

In the introduction he reminds the reader that he described the archetypes that are met with in any analysis that penetrates at all far below the surface, the first of which was the shadow. Jung expresses himself differently about the shadow and the figures behind it here, in a way that I found very enlightening. I can only urge you to read it carefully for yourselves, if you have not already done so, for my bare outline is particularly inadequate here (par. 422).

Expressed very briefly, he points out that the shadow – looked at superficially – is as much a privation of light as the actual shadow of the body but, as we analyze it, we uncover the highly autonomous figures of the animus and anima. When we observe this pair in full operation – the blind demonic opinions in a woman and the glamorous but possessive seductress who produces moods and unreal sentimentality in a man – we begin to doubt *in our own actual daily experience* whether the unconscious can possibly be a mere substanceless appendage of consciousness and nothing but a deprivation of light and good. (It certainly does not feel that way when one is struggling with one's own animus, and I doubt if anyone who has *really* tried to do this could doubt its exceedingly autonomous reality.)

If one is of the opinion that the *human* shadow is the origin of all evil, one is surprised in analyzing it to find that it also contains many good qualities, namely, normal instincts, appropriate reactions, realistic insights, and creative impulses. At this stage, evil seems a deformation or crippling, a twisting of natural facts by the animus and anima. Then one is inclined to think of this pair as the real instigation of all evil, but one cannot stop short at this realization, for it turns out that all the archetypes have a light and dark side and that the Self itself is a *complexio oppositorum*, for there can be no reality without polarity. We do not know what good and evil are in *themselves*; possibly they simply arise from a need of human consciousness and they may lose their validity outside the human sphere. But if everything God does or allows is "good," then evil also must be good and the whole thing becomes meaningless, but in any case suffering remains and the joyful splendour of the life is certainly shadowed by a dark foil of stupidity, sin, sickness, old age, and death (par. 423).

The perception of the animus and anima seems mostly to be the lot of psychotherapists. Yet anyone who has studied lighter literature will have no difficulty in recognizing the anima, for she is a favorite subject of novelists, especially west of the Rhine. It does not always need the interpretation of dreams to reveal her existence to a man. The animus is more difficult, for his name is legion. But if one studies other people carefully, and objectively, one cannot help seeing how possessed they often are. It is, however, much more to the point to study oneself for there is the place that one can do something about it (par. 424).

There is an especially enlightening passage on this subject in *Psychology and Alchemy:*

> No matter how much parents and grandparents have sinned against the child, the man who is really adult will accept these sins as his own condition which has to be reckoned with. Only a fool is interested in other people's guilt. He will ask himself: Who am I that all this should happen to me? To find the answer to this fateful question he will look into his own heart. (Jung 1944, par. 152)

Although at first we almost always meet the animus and anima in their negative and unwelcome form, yet they have at least an equally positive aspect. Since older times, they have formed the basis of all masculine and feminine deities and, as numina, they work now for good, now for evil. They are a supreme pair of opposites, divided by their opposite sex and nature, but they are also full of promise of union on account of their mutual attraction for each other. The animus and anima stage is correlated with polytheism and the Self with monogamy. Natural archetypal symbolism describes a totality that includes light and dark and, though to some extent it contradicts the Christian standpoint, this is not the case with the Jewish or Yahwistic point of view. The latter seems to be closer to nature and thus a better reflection of actual experience. But nevertheless we must not forget that Manichean dualism was a deadly danger to the early church, and that at least the Christian heretics by no means forgot the natural symbols and we find, as we saw, many natural symbols which are shared by Christ and the devil but even the most important of these have had little or no influence on the dogma (par. 425).

The most fruitful early attempts to find suitable symbols for the Self, however, were undoubtedly made by the Gnostics. Most of them – Valentinus and Basilides, for instance – were simply theologians who, in contradistinction to the ultraorthodox, allowed themselves to be influenced by their own inner experience. The Gnostics and the alchemists, therefore, are a mine of information concerning all these symbols that arose from the repercussions of the Christian message. Their ideas further represent a compensation for the asymmetrical image of God presented by the doctrine of the *privatio boni*, in just the same way as the unconscious is now bringing up symbols of totality in order to bridge the gap that has formed between conscious and unconscious, a gap that is widening to such a dangerous degree that it threatens a complete disorientation or even destruction of our *Weltanschauung* (par. 428).

Jung ends the book by saying that he is well aware that this book is the merest sketch of certain Christian ideas from the standpoint of psychological experience and points out that it lays no claim whatever to being a last word on the subject in any sense. As his chief aim was to point out the parallels or differences between the empirical findings and the traditional point of view, it was inevitable that we should consider the differences in the language of the various times. This was particularly the case with the fish symbol. Here one is inevitably on uncertain ground and must occasionally make use of a speculative hypothesis or attempt to establish a connection. Obviously every investigator should document his conclusions as carefully as possible, but he should also occasionally venture a hypothesis, even at the risk of making a mistake. Mistakes usually lay the foundation for truth, and if one does not know what something is, it is at least an increase in one's knowledge if one knows what it is *not*.

Notes

1. The title of the book is *Aion: Researches into the Phenomenology of the Self* (Jung 1951).
2. For the most part, I have only summarized the content of each chapter, but occasionally I have put in a comment, which I have almost always put in brackets.
3. Throughout the lectures, page or paragraph numbers without further annotation refer to *Aion* (1951).
4. The lecture, given in 1948, was "Über das Selbst" (Jung 1949).
5. In the *Collected Works*, "On Synchronicity" is included as an appendix to "Synchronicity: An Acausal Connecting Principle" (*CW* 8, pp. 417–531).
6. For the diagram, see *Aion*, p. 227f.
7. For the diagram, see *Aion*, p. 231.
8. For the diagram, see *Aion*, p. 236.
9. For the diagram, see *Aion*, p. 238.
10. For the diagram, see *Aion*, p. 240.
11. For the diagram, see *Aion*, p. 231.
12. For the diagram, see *Aion*, p. 247.
13. For the diagram, see *Aion*, p. 248.
14. For the formula, see *Aion*, p. 259.
15. The Tabula Smaragdina is given with a long commentary in C. G. Jung, *Modern Psychology* (1960), pp. 55–63.

Conversations on *Aion*

Marie-Louise von Franz
with Claude Drey

Chapter 14: The Structure and Dynamics of the Self

Chapter 14 of *Aion*: *Researches into the Phenomenology of the Self*, "The Structure and Dynamics of the Self," opens with the following sentence:

> The examples given in the previous chapter should be sufficient to describe the progressive assimilation and amplification of the archetype that underlies ego-consciousness. (par. 347)

Claude Drey: By "progressive assimilation," does Jung refer to what he said earlier (at the end of chapter 12 of *Aion*):

> In conclusion, I would like to emphasize once again that the fish symbol is a spontaneous assimilation of the Christ-figure of the gospels, and is thus a symptom which shows us in what manner and with what meaning the symbol was assimilated by the unconscious. In this respect the patristic allegory of the capture of Leviathan (with the Cross as the hook, and the Crucified as the bait) is highly characteristic:

> a content (fish) of the unconscious (sea) has been caught and has attached itself to the Christ-figure. Hence the expression used by St. Augustine: "de profundo levatus" (drawn from the deep). This is true enough of the fish; but of Christ? The image of the fish came out of the depths of the unconscious as an equivalent of the historical Christ figure, and if Christ was invoked as "Ichthys," this name referred to what had come up out of the depths. The fish symbol is thus the bridge between the historical Christ and the psychic nature of man, where the archetype of the Redeemer dwells. In this way Christ became an inner experience, the "Christ within." (par. 285)

Marie-Louise von Franz: Yes. You see, there are two processes. Suppose, for example, you want to interpret an archetypal dream. You would amplify. Your patient has a dream about a goat, and you consult many books to learn what you can about a goat. This is what we call amplifying. Now, the other process is that the archetype does the same thing himself: he amplifies himself. This we call assimilation of the archetype. For instance, there is the archetype of the fish in the sea of the unconscious; at the same time, on the surface of the earth, a man called Jesus goes around preaching. The fish says: "This is me." The fish thereby assimilates the figure of Christ. An archetype can amplify itself by assimilating material.

Drey: It manifests itself in man as an assimilation by putting the two together. But what you are saying is that, before these two could come together –

von Franz: – the archetype has said: "Aha! That man Jesus is me. I am going to swallow him." And then men on the surface of the earth begin to say that Christ is the fish. They are influenced by the archetype.

Drey: Is this an archetypal process? Do the archetypes do that?

von Franz: Yes. They relate to each other, they "eat," or assimilate each other.

Drey: Independently of consciousness?

von Franz: Within the unconscious. In the unconscious beyond consciousness. This happens in dreams of religious, primitive representations. Someone has a dream about a snake that eats a bird. Here, the dreamer has not done anything. The snake, which represents the archetype of the serpent, has assimilated the archetype of the spirit by eating the bird. This has happened entirely in the unconscious. If a patient has such a dream, you cannot give him an interpretation that rings a bell for him because the dream content is too far removed from his consciousness. Yet, one archetype has assimilated the other. Ten years later, it might dawn upon him in his consciousness, and then he can relate the dream to something.

Drey: By the assimilation of the archetype, therefore, you mean –

von Franz: – to bring together, to swallow up, to pull up closer or even to take in.

Drey: In other words, the archetypes have a private life of their own and they manipulate man.

von Franz: Yes, they have a private life of their own. Man always stumbles afterwards. For example, we know now from the mythology and from the dreams of modern man that God wants not only to incarnate in his light side, which is Christ, but to incarnate in his dark side also. He wants to become one again. We know this, but eighty percent of mankind do not yet know it. However, their dreams say so, which means the archetype has done it first. It is our task to make the meaning of this real.

Drey: That is an interesting investigation.

von Franz: I know a very personable Christian schoolteacher, who dreamt the other day that the dark brother of God, the eternal snake in the pit of hell, wants to incarnate now. Mind you, this is just a modern man who has not read Jung. But he is told that the dark side of God wants to incarnate in him. He hasn't the foggiest idea in his consciousness just what that means for him. I see that, in about ten years, he will make some discoveries.

Drey: So, "The examples given in the previous chapter should be sufficient to describe the progressive assimilation and amplification of the archetype that underlies ego-consciousness" (par. 347).

von Franz: Yes, that is the archetype of the Self.

Drey: Now, in the examples Jung gave in the previous chapter, was it his intention to show how the archetype actually works? In this book, how does he say it actually works?

von Franz: In this book, for instance, he tells you there has been an old archetypal projection into the sky of two fishes. One fish has assimilated Jesus: he has eaten up the Jesus archetype, and Jesus has become the fish. One might infer that, logically, the second half of Christianity is the other fish, which is the devil, or the dark side of God. Now, you can prove from the writings of Nostradamus that people noticed that now the dark side of God wanted to incarnate. And then came the alchemists, who made a counter-Christ, a material counter-Christ called the lapis, and they called him, too, the fish.

Drey: That is the material lapis.

von Franz: The material lapis is the other fish. Jung shows that, in 1200 A.D., it dawned on the alchemists that the Christ fish and the lapis fish are two aspects of the same thing. All this proves that there is an enormous age-old process going on over thousands of years which works and goes on by itself according to its own law. However, the process influences our consciousness and therefore it is important for us to know. For instance, it is important for modern man to know that we are now in the age of the second fish. Otherwise, he is not in tune –

Drey: – with his time.

von Franz: With the processes of the archetype underneath. Otherwise, he is a kind of anachronism and belongs to the Middle Ages. There are such people today, and they get into endless trouble. The other day a clergyman came to see me. He is really an early-age Christian; I did not know what to do, because you cannot modernize him artificially. On the other hand, in his parish and everywhere he gets into all sorts of trouble. I finally talked him into retiring to a remote rural district, because people there are still lagging behind the times. There, he is still modern. In a city, however, he cannot function, because he is a medieval man and gets into constant trouble. So I thought that if he went to a small remote farming village where people are still medieval, he would be in his right milieu. But he would still be out of tune with the present times. And that's how he is. He is an old man, and you cannot change him. So it is all for the best. He is going to a backward area, where he will not feel –

Drey: – where the majority of people are like him –

von Franz: – are like him, and he will not notice the anachronism so badly. But if he remained a city clergyman, he would be constantly bucking himself and lagging behind the times. Now if he were a young man, I would wake him up and say: look at the big world clock. We are in the second fish. You cannot be a medieval man anymore. But he is too old for that.

Drey: Jung then writes:

> Rather than add to their number unnecessarily, I will try to summarize them so that an over-all picture results. (par. 347)

Now, if you wanted to trace the assimilation and the development of the idea of the Self, what would be the various historical stages? Roughly speaking, how would you classify the stages of the Self? It seems to me that in the previous chapters these various stages have been discussed. If I wanted to give someone a synopsis of the previous chapters, how would I do that? Looking at the table of contents, the order is as follows: "Christ, a Symbol of the Self," then "The Sign of the Fishes," then "The Prophecies of Nostradamus," then "The Historical Significance of the Fish," "The Fish in Alchemy" – it is always the fish. He picks on the fish as one of the archetypes –

von Franz: – who changes throughout history. This book is about what underlies the Christ figure, the fish, and the process it has gone through. You see, in official dogma the Christ-fish is more or less the same thing: a marvelous man with locks and a white nightgown who preaches that we should behave ourselves. Underneath, however, there is a tremendous process that has brought that figure to light and which goes on evolving. So the first question is: What is behind Christ? There you come to the archetype of the fish. But the archetype of the fish does not remain constant over thousands of years. It slowly changes. It is not only an image, but a process.

Drey: Yes. And what are the various stages?

von Franz: First, you have the myth of the god-man who is more a god than a man or who is only one god-man. For instance, there was the myth of Gilgamesh, which was still in the Ram age, before that of the Fish. Already at that time you find images of the god-man. Then at the birth of Christ, the god-man becomes a real man: *veri deus verus homo* (true God and true Man) – this is the new dogma. God is a historical man. Before, you have the god-man Osiris and other god-men, but they are not historical figures. They are mythological figures. As to this fellow who lived in Nazareth, on such and such a street, they said he was god-man. At that moment, Christ was assimilated to the fish and this coincided with the astrological age of the fish. This means that the archetype of the fish, which is the archetype of the savior, is the saving thing which comes from the unconscious.

Drey: How come the fish is associated with the saving thing?

von Franz: Because it feeds you, it leads you. Jung brings lots of amplifications: the fish saves the Vedas, brings the light, teaches wisdom. Oannes is the fish god. As something unexpected comes from the depths, it has always been projected onto the fish.

Drey: Something which is alive and meaningful to man. A fish is meaningful to man.

von Franz: It is mainly a teacher of the meaningful new message. So along came a man named Jesus, who lived somewhere and pretended to be the Son of God. Ordinarily, this would have had no effect. He would have been one fool out of many fools, for a lot of people at the time of Christ said they were the Son of Man bringing the truth. But with Christ there was an immediate association. People said: "He is the fish." This means: he is the thing from the depth that can tell us the real truth. People must have had the feeling that this fellow was more real and had something behind him. And behind him was the fish.

Drey: The archetype, so to say, had already made the arrangement.

von Franz: Yes, yes. The archtype had made the arrangement. It had picked on him. And that is why he was so sure in feeling: I am it. He felt that the archetype had picked him and that he was in accordance with the archetype. And the archetype had picked him. But an archetype does not stay put. It evolved into a more and more supporting movement toward spiritualization, ethics, and light. You know: good behavior, repression, and so on.

Drey: How did the fish do that?

von Franz: Well, the fish is a double fish in astrology.

Drey: I mean the first fish. How did he do that?

von Franz: Well, you have those similes from the early Christians: we are the little fish of Christ; we are the thing which is fished from the depth; Christ is the fish which nourishes us at the end of the day. The fish was always interpreted positively. It became a symbol for the new truth according to which you should behave well. For instance, there should be no sexual desires outside of marriage. People felt that, if they followed this, they were fulfilling the archetype's intention.

Drey: The fish's intention?

von Franz: Yes. They felt this was the fish's intention. This was his message, his new message.

Drey: And did people really speak of the fish as being an image prior to Christ?

von Franz: No, they did not speak of it in so many words but they always said: "Yes, Christ is the fish, and the fish is Christ."

Drey: What did they mean by that?

von Franz: They did not know what they meant. It took Jung to find out what they meant. They just spoke about it.

Drey: It came to them?

von Franz: It came to them to say so, as it is with religious truths. You speak them because you are convinced. Yet, you cannot quote chapter or verse. If you question such people, they simply say it is so. That is why they call it a revelation: something that suddenly stands before your eyes but you cannot say why. And Jung discovered why. He discovered that this symbolized a phase in the development of the Self.

Drey: The Self behind the fish and behind Christ.

von Franz: This means that the Self is an enormous wheel which rolls through the ages. It develops and has phases: good phases, bad phases, dark phases . . . . Jung tries to show all the phases. But he covers two of them only, namely, the first fish and the second fish, because our historical knowledge covers only about that period. It is just a tiny fraction of that enormous archetypal wheel which goes on through the ages. Once Jung said: I can intuit what the waterman age will look like but, as for the capricorn age, I haven't even a wild fantasy. We can't overlook the next phase, for we are approaching the waterman age. We have a vague hunch what it may be like. Thus these phases go on over thousands of years, and Jung took just one – the one we know relatively well. And by it he tried to prove that, through the ages, the Self is a long, long process of development.

Drey: "The archetype that underlies ego-consciousness" – does this mean that underlying ego-consciousness there is a moving developing archetype?

von Franz: Exactly.

Drey: Which lives a life of its own?

von Franz: Exactly. It lives a life of its own and rolls on through the ages, changing.

Drey: And our ego-consciousness can only be a small –

von Franz: – the smallest sector of it.

Drey: Now Jung says: "Rather than add to their number unnecessarily, I will try to summarize them so that an over-all picture results" (par. 347). Now here I get the impression that he begins quoting certain authors who speak of the manifestation of this totality. Jung quotes them in the following sequence: first Hippolytus, then Clement of Alexandria, then Monoïmos, and then he gives an example from the Kena Upanishad, and then he gives an example from the Yajñyavalkya. Now, with this sequence and with these examples does he mean to prove the ubiquity and the autochthonism of the Self, or is he alluding again to the development you just mentioned?

von Franz: No, he is showing the ubiquity and showing that other people have also gotten a hunch that this great, age-old process exists. For instance, I recall Monoïmos, who says: realize for a minute what thinks in you, what sleeps in you, what yawns involuntarily, what suddenly has a thought. Then he says: this is a little doctor and this doctor is God. So it means: I always have the illusion that I think, and so on, but I don't do all this. You don't go to sleep! You can't go, if *it* does not want. You have to take a pill if God does not want to sleep. So there is an enormous involuntary life process in you which you are the expression of. You open your mouth, you yawn and say: Oh! I've got an idea! You have not made all this. It lives in you. It is a very simple thing. Monoïmos realized this. There is a life in us which moves our hands, makes us yawn and makes us think. That thing is a unit, and that unit is God.

Drey: And that unit undergoes a process. This is important. You see, I understood there exists "something" within me which was independent of me but now we add the idea that this thing which exists independently, also undergoes a historical change.

von Franz: Exactly. A very slow historical change. You can put it very simply: it boils down to the realization that God is developing.

Drey: Is this a hypothesis?

von Franz: It is a speculation. You can say that, from the things you see, it looks like that. You cannot say it is so. You can only say it looks "as if."

Drey: The idea that God is developing gives a lot of meaning to oneself.

von Franz: For instance, it is the same thing with the theory of evolution. You cannot prove absolutely that we have developed from one-cell algae. But from all the evidence it looks very much like that. Fossils and our way of developing in the mother's womb give us hunches which seem to say that we have developed from one-cell algae through millions of ages. Thus you can say that, from all psychological documents, it looks as if God, passing through us over millions of years, is developing toward new forms of consciousness.

Drey: Behind everything that goes on is God, who is always evolving.

von Franz: He is not standing still. He is changing and evolving –

Drey: – like a great experimenter.

von Franz: It implies an evolving creation and an evolving God-image.

> In Monoïmos, who was called "the Arab," Indian influences are not impossible. His statement is significant because it shows that even in the second century the ego was considered the exponent of an all-embracing totality, the self

> – a thought that by no means all psychologists are familiar with even today. (par. 350)

Drey: "His statement is significant because it shows that even in the second century the ego was considered the exponent of an all-embracing totality, the self." Jung does not mention "process."

von Franz: No, there he does not. He merely refers to documents which show that people at that time understood that the background of what they felt is something different. The idea of the evolving God-image came only with alchemy. The alchemists saw that it was evolving. The others had not realized that.

Drey: I see. The idea of historical evolving came with alchemy.

von Franz: The alchemists realized that it was evolving, that it was changing. Others only realized that there is something behind our ego which is divine. The alchemists realized that, too, but added that it undergoes a process. They also had the genius to say that not only is it evolving but we have to support it. We should not merely notice that it is evolving but should try to support it.

Drey: To be in tune with it.

von Franz: To be in tune and to support its evolution.

Drey: Now, these early Christians saw that the ego is an exponent or an instrument of the Self. Are these the earliest?

von Franz: Yes. The earliest written sources where they notice it and say, I feel that way.

> Though differently constituted, the two quaternios express roughly the same idea, and in what follows I shall try not only to relate them to one another psychologically, but

> also to bring out their connection with later (alchemical) quaternary structures. (par. 358)

Drey: Jung speaks now about the paradise *quaternio* and the Moses *quaternio*. Just to make it clear to myself: we have the Moses and the shadow *quaternios*. They are two Gnostic *quaternios*, right?

von Franz: Yes.

Drey: Now the lapis *quaternio* is an alchemical *quaternio*.

von Franz: Yes.

Drey: And the paradise *quaternio* – what is that?

von Franz: It is a biblical *quaternio*. You will find it also in other Gnostic texts.

Drey: It is also a Gnostic *quaternio*. So that there are three Gnostic *quaternios* and one alchemical *quaternio*. Is that correct?

von Franz: Yes.

Drey: They are not two and two. They are three Gnostic and one alchemical?

von Franz: Yes, but you must not forget that the origin of alchemy goes back to Gnostic tradition. For instance, Zosimos was a Gnostic alchemist. Alchemy is the continuation of Gnosticism into matter.

Drey: Now when Jung says: "their connection with later (alchemical) quaternary structures" – he is talking about which ones in this book?

von Franz: By "later" he refers to the Platonic Liber Quartorum which contains a "later" alchemical *quaternio*, and he refers also to the Kircher *quaternio* which is also a later alchemical *quaternio* (see par. 414 and par. 416).

> For the ordinary man, these two represent the "royal pair," which for Moses corresponds on the one hand to his "higher man," and on the other hand to his anima, Miriam. (par. 360)

Drey: Now comes an interesting point. Speaking about the ordinary man at that time, Jung points to the relationship between the lower Adam, Moses, and Zipporah, and then between higher Jethro and Miriam.

von Franz: Yes. That is correct.

Drey: First of all, he mentions the lower Adam which refers to the ordinary man in the street, the average Jewish person who lived at that time.

von Franz: Yes. You and me. We are all children of Adam, and I am a child of Adam and Eve.

Drey: Did the Gnostics actually make these designations?

von Franz: Yes, Jung derived them from Gnostic texts. The Gnostics did not formulate them exactly that way. Jung derived them from several sources. One text says Moses is the higher man above Adam and the other texts say this and that, and he put them all together. Those *quaternios* existed in Gnostic texts. Jung put them together.

Drey: Is it therefore a fact that the ordering into *quaternios* is exclusively Jung's idea or is it used consciously by other authors, too?

von Franz: It is used by many other authors. For instance, Markos the Gnostic.

Drey: Did the Gnostics actually use *quaternios*?

von Franz: They used quaternary systems.

Drey: And how did they arrange them?

von Franz: For instance, they said that in the beginning there was a father, a mother who created two sons and two daughters: life, gnosis, reflection, and mind. They generated another *quaternio* and then whole chains of myths always in groups of four. And they do this when they describe the generations of divine division. As for these diagrams, Jung derived them from texts. He found that one text mentioned a higher Moses and the other a lower Adam. Jung put them together into the *quaternios*.

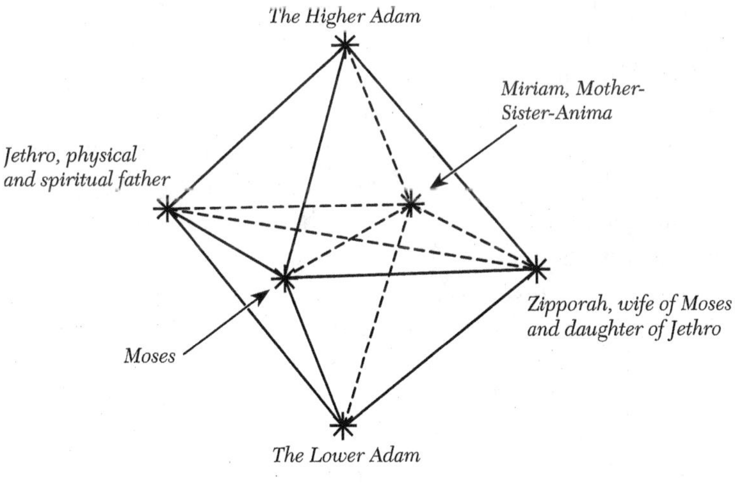

Drey: Now, the ordinary man experiences Moses and Zipporah as his "royal pair," as his higher father and his higher mother. And then Jung says that one of them, namely Moses, has also a higher pair called Jethro and Miriam. Why does he suddenly continue by mentioning the "royal pair" of Moses, that is, Jethro and Miriam?

von Franz: Jethro is the father-in-law of Moses. Moses had not only a wife, Zipporah. He had also a love affair with an anima figure, Miriam, whose father was Jethro.

Drey: Yes. But psychologically, what does that mean?

von Franz: For instance, you dream of a wise old man. Let us say you dream about Jung. And then you would dream about Mrs. Jung. Then you would say: these are now my royal parents who stand in place of my personal parents. The father figure is projected onto Jung: he is the higher man according to whose patterns I try to behave. Then you dream of Mrs. Jung and you would say she is now my corrected mother-image – my mother was deficient. She is a kind of ideal mother-image showing me a pattern of femininity and motherhood. Then you dream that Jung has an affair with a sort of heavenly lady. Dreams could easily produce that. Jung appears in your dream with a beautiful lady who is not his wife. Then you would say: the Self or the wise-old-man archetype has two women. He has a wife relationship and a love relationship. Jung even said you could continue with that development forever. Why shouldn't the Self have a shadow? Why shouldn't the Self have an anima? Why shouldn't the Self have a father? They are chain connections. Rather than continuing to speculate, Jung said: I stick to what I can see in texts and material. I do not speculate on them. You could say, for instance, pointing to a dream figure, that is the anima of the Self. That would mean a feminine power connected with the Self. But this becomes very abstract. In the biblical material there is the account of the higher Moses who had a wife named Zipporah and who also had a love affair with Miriam. She is described as a marvelous woman, who has a kind of priestlike father. Jethro is a kind of father-in-law to Moses.

Drey: Let me go over this once more. Let us say I dream of a higher figure –

von Franz: – and then you dream of the wife of that higher figure, and then your analyst later tells you: well, that is the feminine aspect of your Self. And then you dream of another wife.

Drey: What would that mean psychologically?

von Franz: Psychologically, you could say in abstract language that it is another feminine aspect of the Self, which is again a sublime whole anima figure – a sublime mother.

Drey: Could you say that it is a further and further refinement, and that every chain connection forward is a refinement of the original figure? Or would it be just a further differentiation?

von Franz: It is a further differentiation. You could say, for instance, that the Virgin Mary has the two aspects: in one way she is a mortal woman who had an illegitimate child by God and is therefore the archetype of a mortal woman who gave birth to a divine or half-divine being. But later, in church speculation, Mary was identified with Sophia. Sophia was the wife of God since the beginning of days. For instance, in the Book of Wisdom Sophia says: I played in front of you, before you brought about the Creation (see Jung 1952a, par. 609). So you can say that she is the Virgin Mary, who has these two aspects: she is the mortal wife of God and she is the sublime Goddess who has always been with God. You could describe the Virgin Mary as being two different women.

Drey: Two different names.

von Franz: Yes, two different names. You would have Zipporah and Miriam: they are two bridal aspects of God (the Self).

Drey: Is that a common psychological phenomenon of modern man?

von Franz: Modern man rarely goes so deep into the experience of the Self that he sees that much of it. You have to go very deep into the actual living phenomenon of the Self before you become aware of all those subtleties. For you, your hand consists of bones, flesh, and skin. But if you are a neurophysiologist and dig deeper, you see how complicated it all is. There are not just bones, flesh, and skin. Those are coarse descriptions. Within your hand there is an infinite mystery.

Drey: Did people ever investigate the Self that deeply?

von Franz: Some did, but very few. There were deep mystics and thinkers in the past, for instance the Gnostics.

Drey: I am speaking about modern times.

von Franz: Among our moderns who penetrated the structure of the Self in all its different aspects, it would be hard to find more than three pupils of Jung who did that to any degree. But Jung penetrated the structure of the Self. This book (*Aion*) is the result.

Drey: So there *is* a possibility of going into those figures which represent or manifest the Self.

von Franz: Yes. You could say that these upper figures in the diagram, such as Jethro, are a sublime aspect of the Self which you admire and which guides you. All the lower figures in the diagram represent the Self when one suffers from its disagreeable aspects. But instead of just suffering, one goes into it deeply and asks what is it and how it is. And then you get into all these complicated structures.

> But since Moses is related to Jethro as the lower Adam, or ordinary man, is to Moses, the quaternio cannot be understood merely as the structure of Moses' personality, but must be looked at from the standpoint of the lower Adam as well. (par. 360)

von Franz: Yes, now look at your drawing. If you look at it from Moses' point of view, then you can say: that is his anima (pointing to Zipporah), that is his sublime anima (pointing to Miriam) and that is the wise old man behind his sublime anima (pointing to Jethro). But then you take Moses as if he were an ego, and that is wrong. So you have to look from here (pointing to lower Adam) and then you must say the whole block up here is an aspect of the lower Adam's Self. All four (Moses, Zipporah, Miriam, higher Jethro) are aspects of the Self of this lower Adam. This means that when this lower Adam looks at the archetype of the Self who rules his life, he will discover that they are really four.

Drey: They are continued pairs and different aspects of the Self.

von Franz: You see, all these expressions like the "Self" and so on are only a way of speaking *grosso modo* to give that block of experiences a name and characterize it. But when you look at it a bit more accurately you see that it is not only a block but contains subdivisions. It has different aspects.

> From this we can see that the Naassene quaternio is in a sense unsymmetrical, since it leads to a senarius (hexad) with an exclusively upward tendency: Jethro and Miriam have to be added to the above four as a kind of third storey, as the higher counterparts of Moses and Zipporah. (par. 361)

Drey: Now the senarius as I drew it would be Adam and Eve, Moses and Zipporah, higher Jethro and Miriam.

von Franz: No. Eve is to be left out.

Drey: Why?

von Franz: For the moment she is not part of the discussion. We are concerned only with Adam and with his analysis.

Drey: But Jung mentions the lower Adam, Eve, Moses, Zipporah, Jethro, and Miriam (par. 360).

von Franz: Yes. He has put it here that way. But from the point of view of Adam and referring to the drawing (par. 359), you can also take: the lower Adam – Moses, Zipporah, Jethro, Miriam – and the higher Adam. But I see, Jung has not considered this drawing. The whole thing is a rhythm of either six or four. You can either begin here and count these six, or you can begin there and count those six. But it is always a rhythm of six which includes an unfolding into a four.

Drey: Isn't it always a rhythm of two-two-two?

von Franz: No. It is a one-four-one-four structure and not a structure of two-two-two-two and so forth. You could arbitrarily subdivide it into two-two-two. In the I-Ching, for instance, there are texts subdivided into two-two-two and so forth.

Drey: What is the difference between them and what is their similarity?

von Franz: That has never been fully determined. From my own number study, however, I would say that, if you look at the two-two-two-two structure, you are looking at it from the standpoint of matter, and if you look at a structural rhythm of one-four-one-four-one-four, then you are looking at it from the standpoint of totality. In the material world it appears as two-two-two, but in the psychic structure it is actually one-four-one-four-one-four and so forth. Six contains both rhythms: three times two, or four plus two.

Drey: In the analytic situation, you mean two in the one person and two in the other person, because there are cross-correspondences between the conscious and the unconscious of two people who meet.

von Franz: Yes. For instance, if two of us sit in a room and discuss with each other as we are now doing, we are four people: you and your anima and I and my animus.

Drey: Correct.

von Franz: That is why you practically always have two-two-two-twos when you sit in a practical situation and when you relate to each other.

Drey: When you take the unconscious into account, since there are two conscious personalities and two unconscious personailities –

von Franz: Your ego, my ego, and your unconscious, and my unconscious. There are four people in the room.

Drey: Is that how it is?

von Franz: Yes.

Drey: That is what makes it a four-four-four-four and so on instead of a two-two-two-two. Is that correct?

von Franz: Yes.

Drey: And if there are two more people in the room, then there is another four. Is that correct?

von Franz: Yes. It is always a rhythm of fours.

> From this we can see that the Naassene quaternio is in a sense unsymmetrical, since it leads to a senarius (hexad) with an exclusively upward tendency: Jethro and Miriam have to be added to the above four as a kind of third storey, as the higher counterparts of Moses and Zipporah. (par. 361)

Drey: "From this we can see that the Naassene quaternio is in a sense unsymmetrical." What does Jung mean by "unsymmetrical"?

von Franz: I shall explain "unsymmetrical" with an experience of Pauli. He made a drawing from a dream as follows:

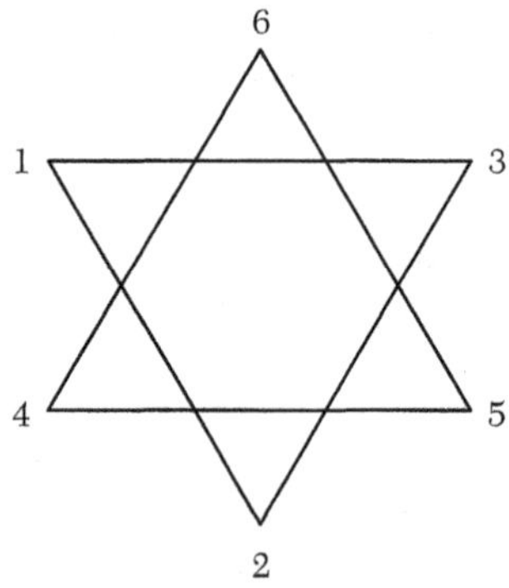

He drew six points and then six identical lines: lines 1–2, 2–3, 3–1, 4–5, 5–6, and 6–4. Then he said that the anima in the dream told him: no, it is not this way. And the anima made a new drawing in which you have four points and four lines:

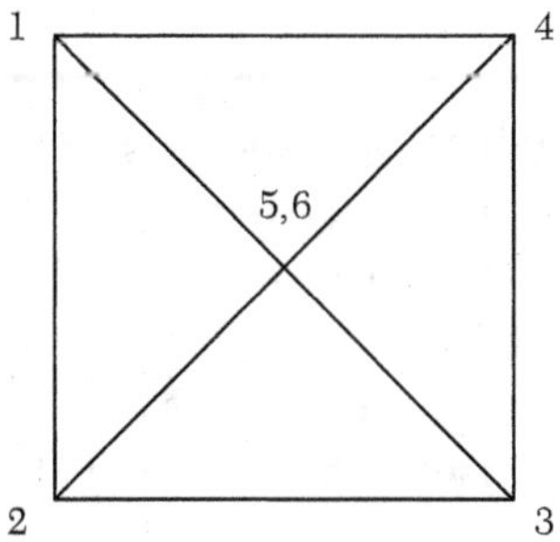

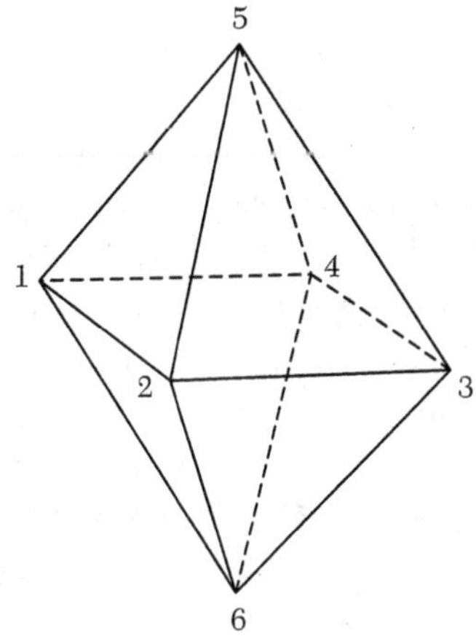

Lines 1–2, 2–3, 3–4, and 4–1. And then the anima connected the points 1, 2, 3, and 4 into the apexes 5 and 6. So that, looking at it from the side, you have a double pyramid. And then the anima said that this line, for example, line 3–5, is not of the same length as that line, for example, line 4–3, and that, mathematically speaking, it expresses an irrational relationship. And then the anima concluded: therefore the six rhythm does not consist of six identical lines. It consists of six points but all the lines are not identical. The rhythm is therefore asymmetrical because the lines connecting to the apexes 5 and 6 are longer than the horizontal lines connecting the base points of the pyramid. Therefore the rhythmic structure is *not* symmetrical. The six rhythm consisting of one-four-one-four-one-four and so forth is asymmetrical. The anima also said that this is where "time" comes in, because otherwise there would be no movement.

Drey: But what does this mean psychologically?

von Franz: Psychologically it means that, if everything is in balance, then it does not move and there is no "time." It remains eternally the same. It takes an imbalance and an asymmetry to make life go on.

Drey: When the *quaternio* results from the One (point 5 or point 6), isn't that an imbalance?

von Franz: No, for then you would have harmony. You have One, and when it goes into the *quaternio*, you have harmony. But because there is an imbalance, the movement continues into a One and then again into a *quaternio*. It takes a certain amount of imbalance to make things go on. You see, the *quaternio* is in itself a balance and the apex (the One) is in itself a balance, but the apex (the One) is asymmetrical to the four points (the *quaternio*). The *quaternio* (the four points) pulls this apex down and then, in order to put it right again, you have to have another movement toward the apex (the One) because, otherwise, you would stay here in the *quaternio* (the four points), in that harmony of the four.

Drey: By "unsymmetrical," what does he mean?

von Franz: He means that the horizontal lines are mathematically not of the same lengths as the lines connecting to the apex.

Drey: And, psychologically, it means –

von Franz: It means, for instance, that the ego – even the individuated ego – can never really express the original Oneness. There is always a slight imbalance. Let us say that you are completely individuated. You are still not representing your own Self completely. This is not possible. Therefore, there is still a slight imbalance, or asymmetry. The original Oneness, the original unit of your personality – your Self – is still different from and greater than even the most individuated form of your Self. There is a slight dynamic tension therefore, and that makes the process go on. Asymmetry makes dynamic tension. It is not quite balanced, because if something is in complete equilibrium, it does not move any more.

> Just as the Apophis-serpent was the traditional enemy of the Egyptian sun-god, so the devil, "that ancient serpent," is the enemy of Christ, the "novus Sol." (par. 366)

Drey: What was the Apophis-serpent?

von Franz: That refers to an Egyptian myth which speaks of an enormous serpent in the underworld. The sun-god circulates over the sky; he goes up in the east and circulates in a ship over the sky. He goes down in the west and then, according to Egyptian mythology, he goes into the underworld and comes up again in the east. And when he goes into the underworld, he is attacked each night by the Apophis-serpent.

Drey: Which tries to do what?

von Franz: It tries to block the sun-god out. And then he fights the serpent and emerges victorious again in the east.

Drey: Does he kill the serpent?

von Franz: According to one myth, he kills or overcomes it. It is an eternal process, because the serpent attacks again each night.

Drey: I see, just as the Apophis-serpent is the traditional enemy of the sun-god, so the devil – that ancient serpent – who has to be fought again and again, is the enemy of Christ.

von Franz: In the biblical book of Revelations the dragon is overcome at the end of days. And do you know what happens to the dragon? He is imprisoned in a pit for a thousand years, which means that after a thousand years, the dragon will still be there again. It is the same old story going on and on.

> From this we can see clearly that the serpent was either a forerunner of man or a distant copy of the Anthropos, and

> how justified is the equation Naas = Nous = Logos = Christ = Higher Adam. (par. 367)

Drey: Now he equates the snake Naas to the spirit Nous, to Logos, to Christ, and to the higher Adam.

von Franz: Yes, that is the teaching of the Gnostic sect of the Ophites.

Drey: But Naas is the lowest. How is it possible for them to equate Naas to those higher forms?

von Franz: Well, according to the Gnostics, the serpent appears as the lowest, the enemy of God, who told Adam: if you eat the apple, you will recognize good and evil like God. So the serpent led to the discrimination of good and evil and to godlikeness. Christ also leads us to the discrimination of good and evil and to godlikeness. Thus the serpent in the Bible functions in exactly the same way as Christ. That is not our discovery, for the Catholic Church has already said: if the serpent had not seduced Adam and Eve, Christ could not have been born to redeem us. Therefore, the serpent is the beginning of the work of redemption.

Drey: It begins the discriminating process.

von Franz: Therefore, it is really the same force.

> This appears as early as the fifteenth century in the alchemical Codex Ashburnham 1166, and in the sixteenth century Mercurius was identified with Hermes Kyllenios. (par. 367)

Drey: Who was Hermes Kyllenios?

von Franz: Kyllene is a mountain place in Greece. Hermes Kyllenios is simply the name of Hermes, the Greek god, who was worshipped in Kyllene: a phallic god and a redeemer.

Drey: Do you understand the corresponding footnote?

von Franz: That is a medieval poem: "You too, Cyllenian, this bold enterprise / Fail not, the stream from whose pure spring supplies. [This simply means: Mercurius, don't fail in this bold enterprise, namely, the alchemical work.] The silver men call 'quick,' the primal state / And first beginning of a work so great" (par. 367, note 28). This refers to Mercurius, to the god Mercurius, who is the serpent and who is Hermes and, therefore, the serpent and the wisdom of nature and, as we would say, the wisdom of the unconscious. It is a prayer to that "wisdom" so it will not fail the alchemical work. And that is also the *prima materia*. This means the god who guides the alchemical work is his own material. That is the crazy part about it. You work for God on the God-material.

Drey: That is the paradox.

von Franz: That is the paradox of alchemy. Hermes Kyllenios is simply the god Hermes of Kyllene who is worshipped as a creative god. It is simply an ancient name for Hermes Mercurius.

> It is significant that Gnostic philosophy found its continuation in alchemy. "Mater Alchimia" is one of the mothers of modern science, and modern science has given us an unparalleled knowledge of the "dark" side of matter. It has also penetrated into the secrets of physiology and evolution, and made the very roots of life itself an object of investigation. (par. 368)

Drey: What is meant by "the very roots of life itself"?

von Franz: This simply means that modern science wants to know how there originated, out of inorganic matter, our entire planet, the first living cell and, through evolution, man. You see, modern materialistic theory thinks that we have come from one alga in the ocean. There was a first living molecule which perpetuated, and scientists are investigating this and, so to speak, the dark side of man, how he originated physiologically; and they go back to the first alga in the ocean. This is the meaning of "the roots of life."

Drey: Would we say that the archetypes are the roots of life?

von Franz: We Jungians would say that. Behind the first alga was the archetype. When, out of the primordial ocean, the first alga began to pulsate and live and perpetuate itself and from it came plants and animals over millions of years – we would say this took place under the guidance of the archetype.

C..D.: Is life therefore a manifestation of an original archetype?

von Franz: Yes. Jung does not dare to say that, but we can infer it from what he says. That is why he says in his book on synchronicity that it looks sometimes as if the archetypes are not only psychic structures but are world-creating structures as well. That is, the archetypes are not only structures of our unconscious but are structures of the whole universe. Jung goes on to say: it looks as if it were so . . . . I think that the more one investigates, it does look as if it were so.

> In this way the human mind has sunk deep into the sublunary world of matter, thus repeating the Gnostic myth of the Nous, who, beholding his reflection in the depths below, plunged down and was swallowed in the embrace of Physis. (par. 368)

Drey: Now, what does Jung mean by "sublunary"? Shouldn't he say the lunary world of matter?

von Franz: Sublunary, simply. You see, in ancient times people thought that below the moon lies the material mortal world and above the moon lies the spiritual world.

Drey: The moon revolving around the earth created a circle and, out of this circle, a sort of dividing sphere was formed.

von Franz: Yes. A dividing sphere. Therefore he says "sublunary world," which signifies simply what we know today as our material mortal world, our physiological body and its surroundings – all of which is transient.

> As Hippolytus says, the Gnostics identified the serpent with the spinal cord and the medulla. These are synonymous with the reflex functions. (par. 369)

Drey: Now we comc to two opposites: the *Anthropos* and the snake. Jung says: "the Gnostics identified the serpent with the spinal cord and the medulla." Now, if he says that the spinal cord and the medulla "are synonymous with the reflex functions," in what way are they opposites?

von Franz: They are not opposites, for the serpent is both the spinal cord and the medulla, and this corresponds to the sympathetic nervous system.

Drey: The medulla is in the back of the head.

von Franz: Yes.

Drey: I can see why he says that the Gnostics identified the serpent with the spinal cord, but why did they identify it with the medulla?

von Franz: The medulla corresponds to the head of the serpent.

> The second of these quaternios is the negative of the first; it is its shadow. By "shadow" I mean the inferior personality, the lowest levels of which are indistinguishable from the instinctuality of an animal. This is a view that can be found at a very early date, in the idea of the ´ ´
> the "excrescent soul" of Isidorus. (par. 370)

Drey: Now, what does Jung mean by this Greek name, "*prosphyes psyche*," the excrescent soul?

von Franz: One should not say "excrescent." *Prosphyes* means "thrown on to you." *Pros* means "adding" – the "additional grown on to you." I will make an odd comparison for you. Let us say there is a sort of heap of cells on the floor. I sit on it and then I get up. It has attached itself to me, and I notice a big excrescence on my body. It is not really an excrescence, for I have picked it up, and it has added itself to me. Such is a theory of the Gnostics, who identified soul with consciousness. They said that our soul is only what is conscious to us and that we have a kind of additional heap of soul which has grown on to us.

Drey: Which would be the unconscious?

von Franz: Yes. This is why Jung was so delighted with the Gnostics: they had already discovered the unconscious. They called it the "grown-on-to-us soul." One should not say "excrescent," but rather "added on." The word is not translated well. One should call it an "added soul" – one that is additionally grown on.

Drey: And Isidorus is the one who thought of it and described it?

von Franz: Yes, he described it. And Jung was delighted, because this was actually the beginning of a theory of the unconscious: we have a psyche which is conscious and *prosphyes psyche* – an additive, grown-on-to-us psyche which is the unconscious. A lot of historical knowledge is required here.

> In alchemy the snake is the symbol of *Mercurius non vulgi,* who was bracketed with the god of revelation, Hermes. Both have a pneumatic nature. The *serpens Mercurii* is a chthonic spirit who dwells in matter, more especially in the bit of original chaos hidden in creation, the *massa confusa* or *globosa*. (par. 371)

Drey: Jung begins here with alchemy. He says that there are two snake symbols. One is that of *Mercurius non vulgi*, which means "not common." That is the highest Mercurius.

von Franz: Yes. He is a kind of spiritual soul guide.

Drey: The other is the regular *serpens mercurii*, which is a chthonic spirit, dwelling in matter and original chaos. Is that correct?

von Franz: Yes.

Drey: So there are two serpents?

von Franz: Yes. According to alchemy, it is really the same serpent under its light and dark aspects. You see, this is again the higher quaternio and the lower quaternio. We generally think the unconscious is wise and, therefore, if someone in analysis has a problem, we say: "Let us consult your dreams." Then we follow the wisdom of the dream. We assume that the unconscious is the wise serpent, the serpent of wisdom which guides us out of our life problems. But the unconscious also causes us to have crazy anima projections, crazy shadow projections –

Drey: – and all the complexes –

von Franz: – the complexes and evil drives and perversions. The unconscious is the source of all perversions. Thus we can say the unconscious is also a devilish serpent which leads us into perversion, depression, crazy projections, anima-animus fights. That, too, is the unconscious. Therefore the unconscious has two aspects, two serpents. There are people who follow the serpent of the unconscious until they end up in an asylum, which means chaos.

> The snake-symbol in alchemy points back to historically earlier images. Since the *opus* was understood by the alchemists as a recapitulation or imitation of the creation of the world, the serpent of Mercurius, that crafty and deceitful god, reminded them of the serpent in the Garden of Eden, and therefore of the devil, the tempter, who on their own admission played all sorts of tricks on them during their work. (par. 371)

Drey: Why was the *opus*, as understood by the alchemists, "a recapitulation or imitation of the creation of the world"?

von Franz: That is an old archetypal idea. You find it even in modern physics. Scientists think that if they could find out how matter originates, they would find out the secret of creation. Modern biochemists, for instance, think that if they could make a semen and an ovum, they would discover the secret key to what man is. The alchemists were possessed by the same idea. They thought that, if they could transform matter into gold, they would know the full structure of matter and would thereby be looking into God's secret book and how he made the world.

Drey: Now what kind of archetypal situation is behind this?

von Franz: God! The desire to find out about God.

Drey: It is always the same thing.

von Franz: You see, in modern physics, Niels Bohr said to Einstein: "God does not play with dice." That means that by investigating the opus of God, which is the creation, the world, modern scientists want to find out and get closer to that mastermind who created and invented it all. This is their secret passion, even if they do not know it. I mean, if you can't get to know Jung, because he is dead now, the best way to learn about him is to study his books. So too, if you can't know God directly because he does not condescend to show himself to you in a vision, the best thing is to look at creation. Thus you get an idea that you could get closer to what kind of thing God is. This is the secret passion of the more gifted natural scientists who do not work merely for earning money.

> Mercurius is the slippery, evasive, poisonous, dangerous forerunner of the hermaphrodite, and for that reason he has to be overcome. (par. 371)

Drey: By "forerunner," does he mean the prior stage, that is, the stage prior to wholeness?

von Franz: It is a prior stage of wholeness. This means, for instance, slippery, poisonous stuff. Let us say there comes a patient into analysis. You look at his unconscious, which has given him a depression, three perversions, and whatnot. That is already that patient's Self but in a prior stage. You first have to make the patient overcome that kind of nonsense. He must therefore overcome the early stage of the Self, which is a poisonous stage, in order to develop a bit and come to a wiser stage. This is where man comes in. Man must transform his unconscious, which is devilish or dangerous.

Drey: And the analysis is being done on this poisonous Self, this poisonous Mercurius – right?

von Franz: Yes, yes.

Drey: Then the hermaphrodite is already a differentiated stage?

von Franz: It is a better stage than its forerunner. Not yet the complete stage, but it is a better stage.

Drey: Then comes the stage of the suture and then the stage without suture?

von Franz: Yes. At that point the Self is already improved.

> For the alchemists Paradise was a favourite symbol of the *albedo*, the regained state of innocence, and the source of its rivers is a symbol of the *aqua permanens*. (par. 373)

Drey: But wasn't paradise the place where innocence was lost?

von Franz: Yes. The religious idea, therefore, is that we have to regain our original innocence. This is a religious, Christian idea. That is why, for instance, saints go to paradise at the end of their lives. The alchemists, too, had the idea that creation was once perfect and became corrupted through the devil and the serpent. By working on the material, man brings it back to its original completeness or goodness.

Drey: So for both Christians and alchemists, paradise was not the original state, but the final state, that thing which they tried to reach.

von Franz: Yes.

Drey: Is the *albedo* a symbol for the final state?

von Franz: It is the symbol for a goal. It is not really the final state. The *rubedo* lies beyond it. First they were in the *nigredo* and in the chaos. Finding their way out of the chaos of sin and corruption, they then arrived at the next goal called the *albedo*, which was the regaining of the original perfection.

> The snake symbol brings us to the images of Paradise, tree, and earth. This amounts to an evolutionary regression from the animal kingdom back to plants and inorganic nature, epitomized in alchemy by the secret of matter, the lapis. (par. 374)

Drey: By "evolutionary regression," does Jung mean that, in the process, there is sometimes a regression before one advances?

von Franz: No. By an "evolutionary regression," he means that it seemingly goes back but it is really going forward, as you have in Christianity. Every pious Christian strives for paradise, but he strives for it forward not backward.

Drey: But first he has to sin in order to go to paradise. His sinning is the process of going forward – although seemingly a regression. He learns from the sin.

von Franz: Then he goes to paradise, he goes back to where he was. It is a regression but a forward one. This means that the end-goal is also a return to the beginning.

> As already mentioned, the constitution of the lapis rests on the union of the four elements, which in their turn represent an unfolding of the unknowable inchoate state, or chaos. (par. 376)

Drey: By "unfolding," does Jung mean differentiation?

von Franz: Yes, a sorting out, and through that differentiation, a different aspect.

> This is the *prima materia*, the arcanum, the primary substance, which in Paracelsus and his followers is called the *increatum* and is regarded as coeternal with God – a correct interpretation of the Tehom in Genesis 1:2: "And the [uncreated] earth was without form and void, and darkness was upon the face of the deep; and the Spirit of God [brooded] over the face of the waters." (par. 376)

Drey: The *increatum* is what we call today the unconscious, that which is not yet made conscious. Right?

von Franz: Yes, the unconscious when you discover it, when it is just there. The *increatum* is the unconscious when you find it just there in a human being. Nobody has made it; it is just there.

> This primary substance is round (*massa globosa*, *rotundum*, ˜ ´), like the world and the world-soul. (par. 376)

Drey: Why did they imagine the unconscious as round?

von Franz: Why, it is so nice they did. You see, by their *massa globosa* they meant what we would call the preconscious Self. There comes a Mr. Smith who howls about his sleeplessness. First you inquire about his dreams; you go to the *massa globosa*, and you thereby discover the patient's unconscious. This is already his Self, his main Self. Even the initial dream in his analysis, that only shows the horrible mess Mr. Smith is in, is already his Self.

Drey: Sometimes the initial dream indicates the whole process.

von Franz: Yes, the initial dream indicates the whole process. The Self is already there. It has not yet been made conscious but is there only in latent form.

Erratum

The quotation, page 160, should read:

This primary substance is round (*massa globosa, rotundum*, στοιχεῖον στρογγύλον), like the world and the world-soul. (par. 376)

Drey: The roundness means what? Did the Self manifest itself in roundness?

von Franz: Yes. The alchemists simply made fantasies about what it looked like, and the idea came to them that it must be round.

Drey: In this diagram on (par. 390) could you say that the two pyramids above the horizontal line represent a historical development period for the first thousand years and the pyramids below, a development for the following thousand years?

von Franz: Yes, you could.

Drey: First we have the Gnostics, then the alchemists.

von Franz: Yes.

> In order to give our judgment on A – expressed by *abc* – the character of wholeness, we must supplement our time-conditioned thinking by the principle of correspondence or, as I have called it, *synchronicity*. (par. 409)

Drey: Now, does that mean that, in addition to the space-time and causality factors, we must add the psychological objective factor of the correspondence between inner and outer events, namely, synchronicity? First of all, how is this done practically? Can you give me an example in mathematics or in physics where this fourth factor has actually already been added to it, because I have never seen it done? Theoretically I have read about it, but where was it actually used?

von Franz: Well, for instance, a Nobel prize chemist I know of made calculations to produce a certain stereo hormone. He had the temperature and all the other conditions right in the laboratory, but then the thing did not come off. The crystallizing of this hormone didn't happen, in spite of the fact that it should have happened according to their calculations. As you know, in quantum mechanics and in mathematical chemistry it is always a matter of probability calculations. And then the chemist said to his assistant: "Well, I am too tired. I will go home and take a nap. You stay in the laboratory and watch the temperature and everything." And then he went home and had a nap and suddenly he dreamt that the hormone was crystallizing. He was awakened by the telephone, and his assistant said, "Listen, it has happened." And they never found out why; why it didn't work before and then suddenly it did. It was coincident with his dream in which he dreamt it happened. It was therefore an inner event too. Now, this man is shunning Jungian psychology, though he fishes around it all the time. But he is not reflective, and he does not draw his final conclusions. If you were his analyst, you could show that the crystallizing of this hormone has a complete, symbolic, meaningful sequence in his own makeup, having something to do with his fourth function, feeling, which he represses. There is an inner process, a symbolic process, with its own causality and development. According to the rhythm of that process, the fourth function is to be integrated and the shadow quaternio is to be integrated, et cetera. Then there is a completely different process, his rational thinking, his mathematical-probability calculations, his chemistry and so on, with which he worked on this hormone. But the fellow has never asked himself: why do I do all this; what is happening here?

Drey: Are there people today who, in their laboratory work, take into account this factor, the principle of synchronicity?

von Franz: No, no one yet. Academic training tells people they ought not to do this, that it is crazy. My pupil who is lecturing at the Institute (the C. G. Jung Institute of Zürich), Arny Mindel, twenty-six years old, a physicist from MIT, *summa cum laude*, is the first fellow I know who really takes it seriously. Pauli took it somewhat seriously. He knew about it, but he did not openly admit it.

Drey: Haven't they found yet the actual interrelationship? Doesn't one know why this phenomenon occurs?

von Franz: Synchronicity is just an observable fact. The connection is meaning.

Drey: Has synchronicity ever been expressed in mathematical terms?

von Franz: Not yet. That is what I am working on. You see, Jung thought that, before you could do mathematical experimenting with synchronicity, you should revise your number theory. Our number theory is wrong. Our idea of number is wrong. Wherever people have experimented with synchronicity, for instance, in China where they have a long tradition of experimenting, they used numbers, natural integers. But they took the natural integers in a different way from ours. Now, according to Whitehead or Bertrand Russell, we take the natural integers as quantitative units.

Drey: And how do *they* take them?

von Franz: They take them as individuals, qualitative individuals –

Drey: – with a character.

von Franz: Yes, with a character, with a personality. Now, our great mathematicians Herman Wylie and Henri Poincaré also say this. The other day I read a textbook for college teachers written by a Philip Davis, who says that each natural integer has a qualitative personality. He even makes an illustration of a photograph of people and says it has a specific personality of its own. But the mathematicians don't do anything with it. They state it because it is obvious. It is an observation you cannot honestly deny. Then they leave it aside because they cannot do anything with it. They shrug their shoulders and go on with their probability calculations and their matrices, vectors, and parameters. So before you can make a mathematical model, you have to revise your number theory –

Drey: – and our thinking about numbers –

von Franz: – our whole concept about numbers. That is what I am trying to do.

> What the formula can only hint at, however, is the higher plane that is reached through the process of transformation and integration. (par. 410)

Drey: Now comes the next question. Here Jung talks about the formula ABCD. What does he mean by the words "hint at"?

von Franz: The higher plane of consciousness cannot be made obvious by any scientific means. You can only feel it. It is a spiral and not a circle. The movement does not go in circles; it goes forward in spirals. This means that you always return to the same point but on a higher level. For instance, if you meet a person who has individuated, you can say: "Oh, this is still old John Smith" – completely, in the true sense of the word. He has really remained himself. Analysis has not distorted him. He is still the good old John Smith I once knew, but he is on a higher plane. How can you express this fact? You can only say: "I feel it." There is something more mature, more conscious, more calm, and whatever he was is more intensely there and more real. But you can only hint at it. You cannot put into quantitative terms how much of John Smith is still John Smith and how much isn't. You see? This higher consciousness is something you feel about another person. You have a feeling that this is the same old person but somehow he is more worthy, more intense, more real, more himself. But it is something you can only feel.

> The "sublimation" or progress or qualitative change consists in an unfolding of totality into four parts four times, which means nothing less than its becoming conscious. (par. 410)

Drey: Can you give me an example in which sublimation consists of an unfolding of totality into four parts four times?

von Franz: Take, for instance, the four functions. You analyze an intuitive person who comes for analysis. First, he reads a bit of Jung and then says: "I've got it!" He repeats to you the Jungian ideas, and you get the impression that, after two hours, the fellow has gotten the whole thing. He has gotten it but not fully.

I know that Jung once said to an intuitive patient who came to him: "I don't need to analyze you; you have gotten the point." But after that, he analyzed the woman for twenty years. So you see, she did it with her intuition; that is she got it with the unfolding of A. But then her sensation, what she actually did, how she washed and brushed her teeth, and the like, weren't included at all.

So the second step was that this person had to realize it by thinking. That means if you say to such a person: "Explain that whole thing to me logically," he can't. Though he has gotten it with his intuition, he cannot repeat it to you with his thinking. And to learn it with his thinking is a long process for him. He has to sit and learn and sweat and whatnot. Then he has tremendous inner experiences and "Aha!" reactions, and he says: "Now I have really gotten it." But he has gotten it only through thinking. There are two more functions to go. His morals are still completely untouched. They are still primitive, and he just acts for his own advantage out of conventional decency and so on. Suddenly, it dawns on him that moral action has to be tuned in as well. Then he has tremendous sufferings and conflicts. He feels he has to make sacrifices and do unconventional things against collective morals. Suddenly he says: “Aha! Now I really understand. I don’t think I understood it before. Now I really know what it is.”

But there is still something lacking and that is the fourth step: sensation. And if it is an intuitive person, sensation becomes a hell of a business, because when you come to the fourth function, synchronistic events occur. He might, for instance, have a sexual transference and get the idea: “I must not do it.” Then he feels in his body that it must be done with his body, and he gets dreams that it must be done with his body. Then he gets into a hell of a mess and then he loses the whole process. Each time you go from one step to another you lose everything. Suddenly, a synchronistic event may happen – a miracle. This is the realm of miracles. Then he says, “Aha!” He is deeply shaken. He has really gotten it.

Drey: Then his work begins all over again.

von Franz: You can say he is still where he was on the first day. He hasn’t realized more because, on the first day, he had gotten it with his intuition. But everybody who meets him says: “My! That person has changed completely.” He has become what he always was. Therefore, it is a higher level. It is an unfolding into the four, and it is the same thing.

Drey: What would the qualitative change consist of?

von Franz: The qualitative change consists of that higher plane, that “more consciousness,” that “being more there.” You can say the same old Self is there, but it has a different quality. It is more emanating, livelier, it is more there.

Drey: What is meant by sublimation?

von Franz: Sublimation means simply reaching the higher plane. From the point of view of feeling, if you were asked: “Would you choose the former state or the latter state?” you would say that the latter state definitely has a better quality. And that is what sublimation means. It is an improvement.

Drey: But sublimation means changing into something else, doesn't it?

von Franz: No, sublimation is a chemical expression. It comes from alchemy. Freud took it out of alchemy, out of chemistry. For example, when you boil water, it becomes steam. Steam is sublimated water. It is another aggregate state. Chemically, steam is not different from water. But qualitatively it manifests itself in another way. It has a higher potential. In steam, the water molecules are more alive; they whirl more about and therefore give the impression of steam instead of water.

Drey: And the progressive changes are the progressive stages.

> The formula presents a symbol of the self, for the self is not just a static quantity or constant form, but is also a dynamic process. In the same way, the ancients saw the *imago Dei* in man not as a mere imprint, as a sort of lifeless, stereotyped impression, but as an active force. (par. 411)

Drey: Now, in what way did the ancients see the *imago Dei* as an active force?

von Franz: For instance, the Christian mystics said that the *imago Dei* had a knowledge of its own. It wanted you to do and say things; it pushed you into activity. So it is an active force. It is *not* that you just sit in meditation, look within and find a divine spark, and that it just is something divine in your soul, and you say: "Aha!" and that is all there is to it. That is also the case in Zen Buddhism. The Zen Buddhists experience *sartori* and then . . . so what? It only means they have *seen* the Self.

Drey: They were not moved by it?

von Franz: No, but also they have discovered the problem. They call it the difference between essence and function. One sees the essence of the Self, its being. Then it begins to function. After the greatest illumination or mystical experience of the Godhead, the next morning you have to get up, brush your teeth, put your clothes on, but what are you going to do with the mystical experience? Are you going to relapse into your old state, simply eat your breakfast and pretend nothing has happened? No! You become aware that the thing you have seen tells you now to do this, now to do that. Generally it tells you things you do not like to hear, because you are in the habit of doing things according to your own judgment. If you are humble enough, you attend to what it says. If it should say: "Today get on the telephone and put off all business; go visit Miss So-and-So and tell her you love her" – and you say: "I can't, she will laugh at me; besides, today I have a business meeting" – then you have a conflict. If you are decent enough to obey it, a miracle will happen when you visit Miss So-and-So. Not a love affair – it would not be the banal act, which your ego expects, of tumbling into bed. She will say she had a dream that you would come and something important would happen, but she cannot say what. It would be an absolutely unexpected third thing. Then you go home and say: "Damn it all! *It* wanted it to happen!" If you live the whole day like that, then that thing in you is an active thing. *It* begins to do things.

Drey: Constantly?

von Franz: Constantly! It is a process; it is not a static, luminous spot in your psyche. It is a fiery stream which carries you along.

Drey: I follow that.

> The four transformations represent a process of restoration or rejuvenation. (par. 411)

Drey: What does Jung mean by rejuvenation?

von Franz: Let us take again our example of the intuitive lady who has learned "thinking." When she learns "thinking," she is enormously vivified.

Drey: Why? Is it because she has added something to herself and now feels stronger?

von Franz: No, not so much that she feels stronger. It is just a thrill for her. You see, life consists in being thrilled. As long as you are thrilled and excited, you are alive.

Drey: That is true.

von Franz: And when you say, "Oh, damn! This is the same old rot. I know all that!" – then you are ready for the grave.

Drey: Then what does rejuvenation refer to?

von Franz: To be young is to be in a state of discovering life: when you were young, you were excited about women, beautiful landscapes, a boat ride, and each time you thought: "'This is it!" You feel alive. If you follow that inner thing of the Self, you keep young and ever alive. Thus you are constantly new, instead of being bored and blasé and saying: "Oh, I know all that, it is the same old stuff."

> The analogy with physics is not a digression since the symbolical schema itself represents the descent into matter and requires the identity of the outside with the inside. (par. 413)

Drey: Now, by "the descent into matter," does Jung mean the penetration of the psyche into matter, that is, the interaction, the interpenetration of psyche with matter. Is this the case regarding projection into matter?

von Franz: Yes, when there is a projection into matter, then it happens unbeknown to you.

Drey: Right.

von Franz: But if you work on the projection and if in the process of individuation you follow it up, then you have to fetch your psyche which has fallen into matter. You have to go down into matter.

Drey: What do you mean by that?

von Franz: Well, if you have realized everything psychologically, you must draw concrete conclusions, materially concrete conclusions. You cannot just say: "Oh, it is only symbolic." You can call it symbolic, but you have to get down to the consequences, to material facts.

Drey: And that is the identity of the outside with the inside. The saying goes: As it is on the inside, so it is on the outside. It has to materialize on the outside.

von Franz: Yes.

Drey: That means I have to follow the inside by doing it, by materializing it on the outside. Is that what it means?

von Franz: Yes, I have to make the symbol real in all areas, including the area of my material existence.

Drey: Is it correct to say that "the descent into matter" is represented in the schema (par. 410) by the steps from *B* to *C*? And the ascent is represented by the steps from *C* to *D* to a_3?

von Franz: Yes, yes.

Drey: Now, what is the physical equivalent of the ascent? Is it the concept of the separation of psyche and matter, while the descent is a combination of psyche and matter?

von Franz: No, it does not separate after *C*. It proceeds by taking matter along – how shall I say? . . . It is very difficult to explain, you see, because our time process is still in the descent. We are getting to the turning point only now. It is difficult to give an example. However, let us take a person in the first half of life who is too "high up" in ideals and not the type rooted in matter. For him, the analytic process is a descent into matter. This person has to learn the here-and-now of concrete matter, of the body, of physical reactions, of things he feels in his sympathetic system, and so on. All that has to be considered by him as hints of the Self and realized completely. If he experiences this, if he voluntarily goes into matter, then matter dematerializes in the sense that it loses its heaviness. It loses its being in contrast to the spirit.

Drey: In what way?

von Franz: Well, by way of a simile: in physics, the deeper you go into matter, the more you see it dematerializes. Finally, you have a cloud of energy only, a blurred cloud of energy. And we think that matter is something heavy, something you bump against, but this is not completely true. This is merely the impression material things give us. For instance, in physics there is the borderline problem. Why is there a borderline between the leather of this chair and the air? Because this leather is a cloud of electrons and the air is a cloud of electrons. Why are there such borderlines? The physicists haven't been able to explain it. It is a mystery to them. The problem is now to express it in physical terms, how to define borderlines, because the uppermost electrons of this leather and the lowermost electrons of the atmosphere are identical. In spite of this, we experience a clear-cut distinction between this leather and the air. And mind you, this is one of the greatest problems of modern physics.

Drey: Can't they explain it by different states of aggregation?

von Franz: No, no! That is just a word. If you ask what the borderline is concretely, that we don't know. Therefore you can say that the deeper you penetrate into matter, the more mysterious it gets, and the less heavy and bumpy. It becomes a kind of mystery of the manifestation of energy levels, and the same applies to the psychological process. The more you go into the matter of your own life, the more psychic it becomes.

Drey: That means the more an intuitive type goes into his sensation, the more symbolical it becomes. It even becomes spiritual.

von Franz: Exactly. Quite right.

Drey: So it is not just the carrying out of a chore –

von Franz: – serving this earthy, heavy matter, but this earthy heavy matter –

Drey: – has a connection with the spiritual intuition.

von Franz: Exactly. Thus if one has served this earthy, heavy matter humbly enough, at the end of his life matter and spirit will link and become one. And the contrast between inner and outer, matter and spirit, is ended.

Drey: You said that for an intuitive type, heavy matter can suddenly become symbolical, that is, it is lifted into the spiritual realm. For an intuitive type, this would mean that he should work at the meaning of his hated sensation. However, the time he dedicates to the sensation, for example, by brushing his teeth, taking care of his body – he considers this a waste of time.

von Franz: Yes, but he has to do this with religious devotion, as if it were more than just brushing his teeth.

Drey: It goes beyond mechanical devotion, however, I think it entails finding the symbolic meaning behind the act.

von Franz: Yes, but he must not jump at that with his intuition. I insist that it has to be done with religious devotion until the meaning becomes clear spontaneously. You see, the great danger lies in what I call the grip of the intuition on the sensation. For instance, I explained to you that cleaning your teeth is something symbolic, that because you have a good intuition, you then grasp what it is – you get the concept. But then you have used your intuition again.

Drey: I understand intuitively what you tell me. But if I try to find the answer myself . . . .

von Franz: That is why I say, you have to do it with devotion. You see, you must always try to do it devotedly, until *it* tells you, until your teeth tell you what they are.

Drey: Not the inner voice?

von Franz: Not the inner voice! Your teeth must tell you. And then surprisingly it might boil down to your inner voice, but your teeth will tell you what they are in a very strange and unexpected language, in a way that your intuition cannot grab and run off with it again. You have to be a kind of servant working in the dark, until the light comes on.

Drey: You have to work on those teeth?

von Franz: On those teeth, on your body, on whatever duties you have.

Drey: So the idea of "sublimation," as mentioned by Jung –

von Franz: – is an event, and not something which you can bring forth with your will.

Drey: Take masturbation, for instance. People said that to keep from masturbating, one should engage in some sport – that sort of nonsense. This is not sublimation, is it?

von Franz: No, this is not our meaning of sublimation. That is the ego artificially lifting the drive up to another plane, saying: "I don't want the sex drive forcing me into masturbation, so I tire my body through football." That is ego-programing.

Drey: There is also a numinous quality to masturbating.

von Franz: Yes. Now, if you were to masturbate and be able to ask your penis and your body, when it is in orgasm, what it really is longing for . . . .

Drey: Don't tell me now!

von Franz: No, I will not tell you, but then you suddenly might perceive spontaneously. *It* would tell you.

Drey: Then would you always address the organ itself?

von Franz: Yes, naturally! You kind of feel into it what it wants to say. It would give you the most amazing surprise, and if you can accept it, then the drive toward masturbating might naturally subside. You just wouldn't feel like doing it anymore.

Drey: Does it come from the inner voice?

von Franz: I don't know how it comes but it comes through in different ways. Some people feel it inside, some have a sudden flash of an image, and some hear it as if a voice whispered out of the organ. You cannot predict it. It comes in an unexpected way. You have to open, devotedly open to it, kind of listening with your soul. You have to be patient and not allow your intuition to anticipate. You know, intuitives always anticipate.

Drey: Intuition suddenly brings out an image . . . . is that legitimate?

von Franz: It is, if the image rises spontaneously, but you must stay with the image and ask it what it means. Let the image explain. Let us say, for instance, your penis brings up the image of a beautiful woman. You must not say: "Aha! I know it is an anima problem."

Drey: No, that would be silly.

von Franz: But you must stay with that woman and ask: "Who are you?" or something like that.

Drey: Actually you can do that with every emotion that arises from within.

von Franz: Yes, yes.

Drey: Even during the orgasm?

von Franz: Yes.

Drey: Or prior to the orgasm?

von Franz: Yes, you can learn to talk to your emotions, to your physical emotions.

Drey: You know that to differentiate oneself from those emotional states is difficult.

von Franz: Yes, yes. It is terribly difficult. You cannot talk to the emotions because you are the emotions. The first step is to establish sufficient distance so you can talk to it – objectively, so to speak. First, you must separate yourself from it a bit so you can talk to it, then it becomes objective.

Drey: Yes, I follow.

von Franz: For instance, you are in a rage, but with enough distance from your rage so that you can say: "My dear rage, what do you want to do?" Then you are no longer completely in the rage. You can do that with every emotion. Just move out from it enough so you can say: "My dear emotion, what is the matter with you? What are you driving at?"

Drey: Is there such a thing in active imagination as projecting onto fantasy? Can one project onto fantasy – not just project onto an outer object?

von Franz: Oh, yes!

Drey: Is that true?

von Franz: Yes. I experienced something like that myself. I was in a mad rage, so I did an active imagination on my rage. I saw a black dwarf coming out of the waves of the sea, and I was sure this was my rage. As a matter of fact, I thought this was a personification of my rage, and I went ahead and dealt with it for some time. At the end of the story, it turned out that the dwarf was not my rage at all. It was the personification of a creative urge. And all the time, I had projected onto it, just as I would about a human being, thinking him to be a dirty so-and-so although he is not. So I thought: I know I'm in a mad rage.

I shut my eyes to personify the rage and out of the high waves of the lake came a black dwarf, and I thought: Surely, that is my rage. I had also the feeling that my rage would now do awful things.

I coped with the poor creature. Finally, he revealed himself to be something quite different. I fell out of the clouds, as in real life when you think someone is your enemy or shadow and you later find out he is a nice fellow and quite different from what you thought. You see, my problem was that I projected onto my inner image. I assumed that something was there which was not there.

Drey: The emotion you had should have been a warning that it was a projection and not the real thing.

von Franz: Yes.

Drey: If you are too emotional, it is an indication that something is wrong. Isn't that so?

von Franz: Yes, yes. I was frightened. I was sure the black dwarf was my rage and would take a knife and do things to people, because that is what a rage might do. I expected all sorts of things. But he did not do anything of the kind. So you can project onto an inner image. You can make wrong assumptions and projections about the image which appears in active imagination.

Drey: After one notices the emotion, the first thing is to bring up the image by active imagination. Second, it would be necessary to find out whether one is projecting onto the image.

von Franz: Better still, find out what that thing is in itself, independently of what I assume it to be.

Drey: Would you say that masturbating is a problem for an intuitive type because it is a problem that has to do with his body?

von Franz: Yes.

Drey: Has there ever been an investigation of the attitude of various attitudinal types to the problem of masturbation?

von Franz: No, not that I know. But Hillman has written a paper on masturbation, so you might ask him. I haven't read it, so I could not tell you whether he has noted differences between the types. I know that he has gone into the symbolism of it. However, I am sure and I know from my own practice that, for an intuitive, sex and masturbation are naturally complicated by the fact that they form his main relationship to the body and to sensation. For an intuitive, they have a different coloring than for the other types. They are more important for him, more numinous, and more problematic. They are the gate to the fourth function, which is connected with it.

Drey: Through masturbation one experiences the numinous.

von Franz: Yes.

Drey: You know, in masturbation there is always something missing. The relationship is missing.

von Franz: Yes, the relationship is missing. You see, when you have heterosexual relations, an underlying archetype comes into play. Sex is then experienced as being satisfactory and meaningful.

Drey: Is that the archetype of wholeness?

von Franz: The archetype of the mystical *coniunctio* is present, even if you do not feel it. In masturbation there is also an archetype behind the experience, and that is creation. The archetype of creativeness is archetypally behind masturbation. The only archetypal myth about masturbation is that of a God without a partner who, as in an Egyptian creation myth, brings forth the world through masturbation. There is a different archetype behind masturbation than there is behind heterosexual relations. Therefore, if masturbation is carried out with *coniunctio* in mind, it is unsatisfactory. For the question remains: *coniunctio* with what?

Drey: There is no *coniunctio*. You are left in mid-air.

von Franz: It remains unsatisfactory.

Drey: Now one more question on the subject of neglecting things. If an intuitive type neglects things, for example, writing letters, he represses things. Can one say then, that he represses the fourth function?

von Franz: Yes. Generally, the things you neglect and repress are connected with your fourth function. As I have always said, the fourth function is surrounded by a cloud of laziness. I mean, that if the feeling type has to think, he feels like breaking through the sound barrier. If the thinking type has to feel, then he says: "Ugh!" Generally, the thing which everybody neglects lies in the area of his fourth function. One needs a kick in the pants to do it.

Drey: Symbolically speaking, the repression is somewhat like condemning a thing to hell.

von Franz: Yes, it is like having a kind of ill-tempered rejection of something within oneself.

Drey: Is it worthwhile asking for the symbolic meaning of all these physical activities which one does not like to do?

von Franz: Which one loathes doing and has to make a great effort to get to? Yes, one has to ask.

> The analogy with physics is not a digression since the symbolical schema itself represents the descent into matter and requires the identity of the outside with the inside. Psyche cannot be totally different from matter, for how otherwise could it move matter? (par. 413)

Drey: Now, why does the symbolical schema require the identity of the outside with the inside?

von Franz: Well, we generally associate matter with the outside. We refer to this book here as being "outside." It is a material object. Generally, we think *grosso modo* of the soul as being something "inside," and of this material table here as being "outside." You can say therefore that if, in a synchronistic event, this table here behaves like my own psyche, then there is an identity between outside and inside. Take the example which Dr. Jung mentions in his paper on synchronicity, in which a patient dreams about a scarab. Dr. Jung tells her that a scarab is a symbol of renewal of consciousness. At that moment, a scarab flies into the room and settles near the patient. If you were naive, you would say that what happened outside is like a dream. You sometimes hear people say: "I rubbed my eyes because I thought I was dreaming." Suddenly, something happens outside which belongs inside and which is really like an inner event. Then you say: "Damn it all! Are the outer things part of my dream?" At that point, one cannot differentiate between them. There are outer events which behave like my inner psyche.

Barbara Hannah and I experienced a case once: she analyzed an elder sister who tended to psychologically eat her younger sister and tried to dissuade her from Jungian psychology. The elder sister was a devouring mother type of person who dreamt that she saw three tigers in a barn. Miss Hannah said: "Yes, that is what you are doing. That is the devouring mother in you. You must take this seriously. You 'eat up' people!" Later she went with the younger sister on an expedition. They took a boat and went up the Zürich Lake. Soon they noticed a cow barn and lots of people looking inside. Out of curiosity they went over for a look themselves, and inside they saw three tigers sitting. Imagine – in a Swiss cow barn!

Drey: What?!

von Franz: Three tigers!

Drey: In a Swiss cow barn?

von Franz: Yes! Now it happened like this: they learned that the Knie Circus did not have enough cages to keep their tigers in and had hired a cow barn and put three tigers in it. Imagine walking in Switzerland and finding a cow barn with three tigers in it. And the elder sister had dreamed about that the night before. When this happens, one rubs his eyes and says: "Am I crazy or is this just an hallucination? What is happening?" The outside is like the inside.

Drey: I follow.

von Franz: This actually happened.

> Psyche cannot be totally different from matter, for how otherwise could it move matter? (par. 413)

Drey: What would be a good example of how the psyche moves matter?

von Franz: Let us say there is a Mrs. Smith who gets a letter saying that her son in Vietnam was killed. She suddenly faints. Her blood vessels contract, and she falls to the floor. Now, it is not the material paper which made her faint nor the ink on it. What made her faint was the psychic message: "Your son John died on such and such a date." This moved her psyche and not her body. The psyche made the blood vessels contract. The message is something psychic. It was not the paper and ink which made her faint; it was the meaning of the message on the paper which hit her psyche. Then her psyche caused a terrible physiological turmoil.

> And matter cannot be alien to psyche, for how else could matter produce psyche? (par. 413)

Drey: Now, another technical question: what would be a good example of matter producing psyche?

von Franz: Well, for instance, we know that in the process of evolution first there was inorganic matter and then there were plants and then animals who possessed something similar to a psyche. If we are not prejudiced, we would interpret their many reactions as psychological reactions. Then comes man who is derived from higher primates and anthropoids and who has a psyche. Thus, on this planet, inorganic matter has produced beings with a psyche. The theological explanation is that inorganic matter has produced only bodies and that God has blown a psyche into them. But we do not believe that.

Drey: Oh, you mean that the process of evolution –

von Franz: – has produced beings that consist of matter and psyche. Therefore we must assume that, from the very beginning, matter was something psychoid.

Drey: So you can say that psyche produces matter and matter produces psyche.

von Franz: Yes. Yes.

Drey: We do not know what came first?

von Franz: We do not believe the theological idea that matter produced plants and animals with their own souls, and then one day matter produced a higher ape and God came and blew the psyche into it. That is a poor explanation. Therefore, if you believe in evolution as we do, you can say that matter on this planet has produced psychic beings.

> Generally speaking, these prefigurations can be found in the multifarious stages of the mystic transformation process, as well as in the different degrees of initiation into the mysteries. (par. 414)

Drey: Now, what would be a good example of a mystic transformation process? For instance, when one is sexually aroused, he may look upon the other person as a Godlike figure. Would that be an example of a mystic transformation process? I am referring to the numinous quality of the sex act.

von Franz: For one person, a numinous experience can happen in the sex act, and for another person it can happen .... This morning, a woman over seventy years old came here and said: "I don't know what is happening to me! During the night, suddenly I wake up. Big warm waves come over me, and I feel my capacity to love coming back. This morning, I don't know what it was, but I saw trees for the first time. I saw flowers for the first time. I cannot explain to you the experience completely, but it's like I was alive for the first time." She was completely changed when she came into the room. I said to her: "Gosh! Something has happened to you. You look different from the last time I saw you."

Drey: Can I say that mystical transformation and numinous experience are identical?

von Franz: Yes, but not quite the same. You can say that every numinous experience creates a transformation. You cannot have an impressive numinous experience and be the same afterwards. A man who has experienced God is not the same as he was before. If you really have a numinous experience, it does something to you. It is very bad if you forget it and have a relapse. But normally, people say spontaneously: "I feel changed. Since I have experienced that, I feel different." Thus you can say that numinous experience produces mystical transformation.

> We also find them in the classical as well as Christian trichotomy consisting of the pneumatic, the psychic, and the hylic. (par. 414)

Drey: The Christian trichotomy is related –

von Franz: – for instance, to the body, the spirit, and the soul.

Drey: Is that related to the Father, the Son, and the Holy Ghost?

von Franz: Not especially. But in the Middle Ages whenever they had three things, they related them to the Trinity and said that all good things come in threes. In all the textbooks of medieval psychology, Christian teaching held that man consists of body, psyche, and spirit.

Drey: So trichotomy does not refer to –

von Franz: – the Trinity. No, it does not. Trichotomy simply means being cut into three parts.

Drey: Oh, I see. But that could be confusing. Now we come to the table of correspondences (par. 414). Take column IV, the one on the far right. I wrote down the following:

1. *Sensus* could mean the mixture of our sense perceptions.
2. *Discretio intellectualis* could mean any form of discrimination whether through senses or intellect.
3. *Ratio* could mean the ability to reason.

von Franz: The *Ratio* is the ability to put things into an order. This is this and that is that and this is how it is connected.

Drey: This is the reasoning process.

von Franz: Yes.

Drey: And number 4, *Arcanum* –

von Franz: – is a return to the first one on a higher level, and the whole of that experience is a mystery. *Arcanum* means mystery.

Drey: You would not say that it was the apperception of the reasoning. All of a sudden one catches himself and says: Ah! I am seeing my reasoning.

von Franz: I don't think so. I think that *Arcanum* means more than that. It is a kind of realizing what is happening in the total event.

Drey: The fourth one is really the difficult one.

von Franz: Yes, the fourth one is the difficult one. Well, let us take modern physics as an example. The ego of the primitives, as with the Bushmen, experiences a chaos of sense perceptions. As the ego of man develops, he begins to differentiate. He says "this is light" and "this is water," and he develops a theory about it. That would be number 2: discrimination. Then we come to the beginning of natural science, which would be reasoning, number 3, and proceed right up to modern rational science. This covers all the theories that say matter is constituted in such and such a way. The different impressions are reduced to one order representation. You know that modern physicists always look for the world formula. They think they will find one equation which describes the behavior of everything, of every material form. That is what reason looks for. Then comes number 4; for instance, the realization of Niels Bohr, the quantum physicist – that it all happens only if we observe matter; that our theories are not absolute; that we can't say light is a particle or a wave. If we measure it in a particular way, it is a wave or a particle. But we cannot get either one out of the whole picture. The whole thing is an irrational event. It remains a mystery. That means what we are, and what life is and what our recognizing life is, remains a mystery.

Drey: The whole process then becomes mysterious.

von Franz: I read in *Scientific American* the reason why mathematical formulas are capable of adequately describing the behavior of matter is, to modern mathematicians and physicians, still a mystery. Why it is we can make mathematical equations which fit the behavior of matter – nobody knows. A well-known mathematician said this is a complete mystery. We have not even a speculation of how it could be.

Drey: So the answer to that is?

von Franz: It is a mystery and will remain one. Because the fourth step means you have to stop thinking that reason is the ruler of the world or that, with reason, you can put everything into your pocket. You have to sacrifice reason. There are times when reason must admit that reason is not sufficient; reason must admit that it cannot do a thing via logical reasoning. Have you ever heard of a negative proof in mathematics, whereby you can prove that something cannot be?

Drey: Yes, I have.

von Franz: For instance, you can prove that squaring the circle is not possible. You cannot square a circle, but you can stop people from trying by proving that it cannot be done. Well, that means reason can prove that reason cannot do it. This is satisfactory, because at least you don't try anymore. So it is with the phenomena of life. We must ultimately know that they are beyond reason, and we can even prove this with reason.

Drey: There is another question which I would like to ask you. Jung seems to add to "the proof by numbers" – the quantitative proof – also "the historical proof" – the proof that something happened over a long period of time. Jung always goes into "the historical proof" by reverting to history. You see, scientists say that if they can prove a thing happened so many times, they can assume with certainty that it will happen again. But Jung says this is insufficient for psychology, that we must go back to history. Why is this so? Why does Jung say that we need "the historical proof"?

von Franz: Because the psychological behavior of man changes in history. If you want to find the basic structure, therefore, you have to take history into account. Let us say, for instance, a modern American scientist computerizes the family behavior of the modern American. He will get more or less a patriarchal picture. But if he did this including Africa, and if he did this including Asia, and if he did this including the Egypt of two thousand years ago, he would get a completely different picture. This means that, if you want to find out what is basically human you will have to include history, because if you take only a slice of modern mankind, you don't get the whole picture. Mankind changes. There are fashions and waves of fashions. But those things about mankind that have remained the same for ten thousand years form the basic structures. You see, Jung looks for the archetype, namely, the basic behavioral structures of man, which you cannot find by merely taking tests of modern man. That which remains constant in spite of catastrophies, changing fashions, civilizations, races – what remains the same over ten thousand years – only that can be called a basic human structure. If we take a shortcut, I mean if we consider only modern man, we don't get a complete picture. A change might occur in the next generation.

Drey: So you cannot say that you have found the common denominator until you have taken history into account. Other sciences, for example, anthropology and the like, do that also. They use the same historical principle and don't just dig up graves of today.

von Franz: Modern behavioral science people in America think that by taking twenty thousand college students and computerizing their behavior they have gotten a basic image of man's social behavior, and they publish their findings with great fanfare. I say they are fools. First, they have taken only young Americans; second, Americans only; and third, if they took their test data from Asia or from ancient Egypt they would get a completely different picture. Then they say: "Now we know the basic behavior of average man." They have missed the point. For if you take history, then you see that certain things remain for ten thousand years. Then and only then can you say that such and such is really human. What has been the same pattern of behavior for ten thousand years can more safely be called the human structure than what tests of only modern man reveal.

Drey: That is just a slice of the whole bread. It is not both crosswise *and* lengthwise.

von Franz: And Jung prefers lengthwise. He says the constancy of time is a relative proof of a really basic structure, for certain structures can be changed by political pressure.

Drey: He is interested in the common denominator taken over a period of time. Is that correct?

von Franz: Over a period of time and comprising all races, which means not the white man only. You may find the same basic pattern in the Bushmen, in the Pygmies, in the Asiatic people and in the Firelanders.

Drey: This is very important.

von Franz: Then you can relatively safely say that we are touching a general human structure, one which is really basic to man's behavior.

Drey: This is an important argument, and people tend to forget it.

von Franz: Yes. Behaviorists call us unscientific, but I say we are more scientific than they are, because we take into account a broader material than they do.

Drey: So "numerical proof" is not enough. You have to have "historical proof," too.

> This table of correspondences shows the various aspects of the *opus alchemicum*, which was also bound up with astrology and the so-called necromantic arts. This is evident from the use of significant numbers and the invocation or conjuring up of the familiar spirit. (par. 415)

Drey: Now what does Jung mean by "the familiar spirit"?

von Franz: There are many texts which treat the magical love act. For instance, a young Greco-Egyptian man is in love with Miss So and So, but she does not give him a second look. One night, he kills a black cat according to a certain recipe, and he calls upon a familiar spirit, which may be the spirit of the cat or of the moon goddess. He asks the spirit to assist him in his magic action; he brews a concoction and smears it on the house of his lady. Then he believes that tomorrow she will certainly requite his love and say yes to what she said no to before. There are endless recipes of this sort, and the familiar spirit, say of a god is conjured up to help one with the magic action. All magicians use familiar spirits. For instance, there is the archetype of the Indian medicine man, who never performs an action without first calling upon his helping spirit. He may even have a bear spirit to whom he will say: "I have to go cure Mr. So and So; will you please come along and help." You then hear a whizzing in the air and whatnot. Then he says: "My spirits have now arrived." Then there are the Eskimo shamans who beat upon drums and call out: "So and So, come!" Then they say: "My familiar spirits have now arrived. The ceremony can begin."

Drey: Would Christ be a familiar spirit to the Christians?

von Franz: Yes, a Christian may pray to exorcize and will invoke Christ or the Holy Spirit.

Drey: Would you say that our dreams, in a certain sense, are our familiar spirits?

von Franz: I would say that unknown thing – the composer of our dreams – is our familiar spirit. Not the dreams but the composer of our dreams. Every night there is a fellow who makes up a marvelous story. That is our familiar spirit in whom we trust.

> Similarly, the age-old art of geomancy is based on a sixteen-part schema: four central figures (consisting of Sub- or Superiudex, Iudex, and two Testes), four *nepotes* (grandsons), four sons, four mothers. (par. 415)

von Franz: There is a technicality here. "Iudex" means judge. "Superiudex" means upper judge, or the judge above the other judge. This means the sub-judge, the upper judge, the judge and the two witnesses. They are all configurations of numbers. This is a very complicated thing.

Drey: Now comes the Kircher quotation (par. 416). In this *tetrameria* he goes from stage II, which he equates to ten, to stage III, which he equates to one hundred. This is equivalent to passing from "discriminating" to "reasoning" in the Platonic tetralogy.

von Franz: Yes, there is a parallel here, I never looked at it that way, but it is true. Actually, this group (Platonic tetralogy), which comes from an alchemical book, and this subdivision, which comes from a number theory book, are not directly connected. Both are but examples of fixing subdivisions. However, they are slightly different.

Drey: Could you say "reasoning" is required when one goes beyond ten, that is, up to ten you do not need "reasoning," after ten you do.

von Franz: Yes. But I would not put the two systems together. Because their movements are different. The Platonic tetralogy begins with the chaos of the senses and arrives at the oneness of impressions, and Kircher's system begins with the oneness of the godhead and arrives at the chaotic multifoldness of the ten thousand things. The movements of the two systems are different. One may say that number IV of Kircher's quaternity system corresponds to *Sensus* (number 1 in row IV of the Platonic tetralogy); number III (of Kircher's quaternity) corresponds to *Discretio intellectualis* (of Platonic tetralogy); number II (of Kircher's quaternity) corresponds to *Ratio* (of Platonic tetralogy), and the first stage of Kircher's quaternity, the *Monas*, corresponds to the *Arcanum* of the Platonic tetralogy. You see, Kircher's description proceeds from the godhead downward into matter, and the other text proceeds from a chaos of matter and goes slowly to the realization of the godhead. The Platonic tetralogy comes to us from a natural scientist whose system begins with the *Sensus* and slowly builds to the realization of the mystery. On the other hand, Kircher, who was a Jesuit theologian, begins from God and proceeds to the many.

Drey: Therefore, the Book of Platonic Tetralogies goes upward and the other one –

von Franz: – goes from God to matter – downward. If you keep this in mind, then you can consider them as parallel, but you have to turn one around.

> "When in this way we shall have brought the absolute unity back to the infinitely simple from all perceptible, rational or intellectual multiplicity, then nothing more remains to

> be said, and then the Stone too is not so much a Stone as *no* Stone, for everything is the simplest unity." (par. 417)

Drey: In the above quote, Kircher says, "in this way we shall have brought the absolute unity back to the infinitely simple." Does this mean that after item IV the multiplicity which we find in items II and III has been brought back to item IV, to the unity?

von Franz: Yes, yes.

Drey: Is item IV the new starting point for further discrimination?

von Franz: Yes, yes.

Drey: What would be a good example of this?

von Franz: Well, there would be the thinking type who goes to school and learns all sorts of things. He studies philosophy under a good teacher, and the teacher shows him how he can bring those many things together through reasoning. Then the teacher, if he is a good one, will teach him that all this reasoning and putting of things into order is not the ultimate thing. Beyond this there is a unity of things which one can neither grasp nor put in his pocket. The student feels satisfied, for he now knows how to use his thinking and knows, too, that the transcendent oneness of reality is beyond his thinking. Suddenly he realizes that he can do now the same thing through intuition and through sensation and through feeling. Now let us say, for instance, that he discovers his feeling function. He knows that at breakfast he feels this and at ten o'clock he feels that – a chaos of things. He then begins to differentiate and discriminate: "I feel love and hatred and so on." He begins putting things into order, and finally he says: "Beyond all this there is a unity which I cannot describe." Thus he has used the same process with feeling that he used with thinking.

Drey: But he always ends up with his thinking.

von Franz: He always ends up with his thinking. That is why even the Zen Buddhists say: after you have gone through the whole plane of higher differentiation, you receive the highest illumination. After that you go into the unconscious and you forget all about it.

Drey: Because you give up?

von Franz: No, because you have the humility to know that even the highest realization is not the last. It is an even greater realization to know that the highest realization is not the last.

V.D.: And is that feeling always present?

von Franz: It is always present, for then you know that, no matter how far you go with your inner conscious realization, beyond it lies the greater. That is, so to speak, the ultimate stage, wherein you realize the very limitation of your own enlightenment.

Drey: After the completion of the cycle, Kircher says: "and then the Stone too is not so much *a* Stone as *no* Stone, for everything is the simplest unity" (par. 417). Does this mean that once the Stone has been made, the moment of totality has been reached, at which point the totality is again a unity, it is ready to fall apart again in the next process forward?

von Franz: The totality will either fall apart again, if it still has to be circulated or, in the ultimate stage, which you simply cannot talk about anymore, you must not call it *a* Stone. You see, if you talk about it as *a* Stone, it is again the thing which you can put into your pocket.

Drey: Are you talking about the Self?

von Franz: Yes, about the Self. Then comes the moment when you talk as though the Self does not exist, in order to do honor to the Self, for it is beyond what you can talk about. It is blasphemy to talk about the Self. If you really know what the Self is, you say paradoxically that the Self is and is not, in order not to commit the blasphemy of talking about it.

Drey: There is no more image then?

von Franz: No more image.

Drey: Is that the reason why the Jewish people do not like to make images of God?

von Franz: Yes, yes.

Drey: That is the same thing. They have a great resentment toward making images.

von Franz: Yes. Because they know that as soon as one has an image, he begins to talk and gossip about it. The Talmud scholars and theologians, too, threw it about like an object in their pocket. The really religious introverts who knew it as a terrible thing said: don't make images. You must always keep in mind that the Self is a thing which we cannot realize. Even if we talk about it all the time, we cannot realize God. We may talk about this or that experience, but we cannot realize him in his essence. We must keep this in mind, otherwise we keep on talking as if we knew the Self.

> And even as the absolute unity of that concrete and rational Stone has God for an exemplar, so likewise its intellectual unity is the intelligence. (par. 417)

Drey: We compared Kircher's system with the system in the book of Platonic tetralogies. You said that, whereas the book of Platonic tetralogies starts –

von Franz: – from down the visible world, from the nature world, and then goes upward to abstraction, Kircher's world goes downward: it begins with the concept of God and deduces from him the visible world.

Drey: In other words, Kircher begins with the One and ends up with the many.

von Franz: Yes. According to Kircher's idea we have to make the philospher's stone a concrete thing. In the last stages however, it becomes a spiritual stone. Therefore, he says it is *a* stone and *no* stone. Very often in alchemy you find that the stone in the end is something concrete. The alchemists talk contradictorily. They say that the stone in the end is something concrete and is *not* something concrete. You see?

Drey: Did they actually work physically on a stone and, in preparing it, introject into the stone or project onto it a spiritual element?

von Franz: Sometimes they did. Some did, but not all. Then others had some parapsychological experiences: for instance, levitations or that an object moves of its own, as in a spiritistic session. Then they said the stone was not orderly concrete matter but was what the English spiritists would call "the subtle body," that psychic thing which can move even matter. Some alchemists thought of it as something like that. That is why all the texts contain contradictions: they say it is concrete and it is not concrete; it is something material but it isn't just ordinary matter. That's why they stammer at describing something they really can't quite describe. Because Kircher is a Christian theologian, he, as well as others, simply put it again into the spirit. So, for them, *it is a stone* and *it isn't a stone*; it is the intelligence, meaning by that a kind of capacity. In modern terms, we would call it the capacity of becoming conscious. That is what Kircher means by intelligence. This is typical medieval theological thinking. The absolute unity of that concrete stone, meaning that concrete alchemical stone, is absolutely one. It cannot be disintegrated any longer.

Drey: In other words, any stone would have such a unity.

von Franz: You see, any other stone you can subdivide or dissolve with acid. But the philosopher's stone is something you cannot dissolve with acid. Therefore, they say, because of its absolute unity, it is an imitation of God. Because absolute unity has God as an exemplar, so likewise its intellectual unity is the intelligence. That means it is an intellectual unity: it is one idea. It is one thing. Also, spiritually it is one thing. And that has the intelligence of God as an exemplar. You see, the difficulty with that text is that it had an extensive historical background. For instance, in medieval language "intelligence" means the intelligence with which God rules the world.

Drey: That is, the human intelligence projected onto God?

von Franz: Yes.

Drey: Is that correct?

von Franz: Yes. You could translate it as the meaningfulness man found in creation which he called the intelligence. We think, or at least some of us do, that creation has some meaningfulness to it. We can find traces of it. Well, that meaningfulness would refer to the intelligence of God.

Drey: Yes, otherwise why should there be a meaning on anything, if there were not an intelligence behind it?

von Franz: Yes, exactly. That is what he means there; namely, because the philosopher's stone is such an intellectual unity, it refers to that secret intelligence of God in creation.

Drey: I still don't fully see the analogy there. It is an analogy, isn't it?

von Franz: Yes, it is an analogy.

Drey: He compares the unity, on one hand, and takes God for an example.

von Franz: Yes, because God is one.

Drey: In other words, the philosopher's stone formed itself according to the unity of God?

von Franz: Exactly.

Drey: Is that correct?

von Franz: Correct.

Drey: Likewise the intellectual unity in the human being is like the unity of God and is like the intelligence of God, which means that this intellectual unity in the human being is a form –

von Franz: – is a form of the meaningfulness of the whole creation.

Drey: The intellectual unity in man is to the intelligence of God like the little spark to the big spark.

von Franz: Exactly.

Drey: That sentence isn't easy to understand.

von Franz: Yes, it is complicated.

> "You can see from these unities how the perceiving senses go back to reason, and reason to intelligence, and intelligence to God, where in a perfect cycle is found the beginning and the consummation." (par. 417)

Drey: Also this next sentence is difficult. Now, "from these unities" refers to, on the one hand, the unity of the stone; on the other hand, the unity of God; and third, the unity of the intelligence within man.

von Franz: Yes, right, that is correct.

Drey: You can see how the perceiving senses, with which man perceives what goes on within himself, go back or lead to reason, to the reason of man, and from the reason of man to intelligence which would be the intelligence of the creation, that is God's intelligence –

von Franz: – of which man has a spark.

Drey: The first "intelligence" means man's own intelligence, that is the little spark. By analogy, from man's own little spark one can go back to the much larger intelligence of God, to the spark of God. Is that correct?

von Franz: Correct.

Drey: And then: "where in a perfect cycle is found the beginning and the consummation."

von Franz: It begins with God and goes into the reason and intelligence of the human being and then it lands back in God. That is the perfect cycle.

Drey: Cycle is a circle in time. Like a spiral?

von Franz: Cycle always implies time. For instance, the cycle of the seasons of the year is a circle which rolls on in time – not in space but in time.

Drey: So the cycle means that everything originally began with the intelligence of God. From there it came into the intelligence of man and then to the reason of man, and from the reason of man it goes to the senses, and from the senses –

von Franz: – it goes back to God.

Drey: It goes back to the objects which the senses perceive, to what is again God. In other words, God is the whole universe. Every single little part is then God.

von Franz: Yes, correct.

Drey: What does it mean that the end turns back to the beginning? We know that it turns once more to God. Because the intelligence of man is the intelligence of God. That is the link between the two.

von Franz: Correct.

> (That Kircher should choose the *lapis* as an example of discriminate [*discretae*] natures is obvious enough in terms of alchemy, because the lapis is the arcanum that contains God or that part of God which is hidden in matter.) This, too, is an analogy of our formula. (par. 418)*

Drey: Now, "that Kircher should choose the lapis as an example of discriminate natures is obvious enough in terms of alchemy." Why is it obvious? Could it be because the alchemists projected the individuation process into the lapis?

von Franz: Yes, completely correct. You found the answer yourself.

Drey: "The *lapis* is the arcanum that contains God or that part of God which is hidden in matter. This, too, is an analogy of our formula." Can this analogy formula be related to the drawing (par. 391)? Where would God then be? Would he be the *Anthropos-Rotundum*? Is he included in the drawing? Or can this analogy be related only to the formula (par. 410)?

von Franz: I would say it is included in the drawing. I would say that the *Anthropos-Rotundum* refers to an aspect of God and that the *Serpens* refers to an aspect of God.

Drey: The *Anthropos-Rotundum* and the *Serpens* refer to aspects of God.

von Franz: Yes. You see the *Serpens* is the shadow of God. So you can say the vertical axis represents God's nature and the horizontal axis, the stone and the man, represent man's nature. This is how you can relate the analogy formula to this drawing. The *Anthropos-Rotundum* is the sublime aspect of God and the *Serpens* is the undeterminable dark aspect of God. The Homo – that is the known aspect of man – and the lapis – that is the unknown essence of man. This is how you can relate these two.

Drey: And how is this analogy formula related to the cyclical formula (par. 410)?

von Franz: You could say that whenever God becomes man, God goes through this cycle. You could also say that wherever God manifests himself, he manifests himself through this cycle.

Drey: He puts man through this cycle in order to manifest himself.

von Franz: Yes.

Drey: God puts man through a cycle in order to manifest himself through man's work.

von Franz: Within man's work. That is right. Only after man has gone through the whole cycle does he begin to realize what God is. You cannot realize these things without first doing them. That is why Dr. Jung, if he had an idea not yet worked out, would say: "I let my hands do something, for example, carve a stone or paint, and then I find out what is moving me." You see, this is the opposite to thinking out things in the brain. You do the thing that God moves you to do or the unconscious moves you to do; afterwards you think about what it was. And this is how you discover the real thing.

Drey: Realizing all the time that, while you are working in that spontaneous fashion, it is actually God who is moving you. Correct?

von Franz: Yes, and you have the obligation to meditate on your action afterwards. You see, this is real active imagination. You do the imagining. This means you let yourself be moved by whatever moves you and then you sit on it and sweat to find out what it is. Thus active imagination makes sense only if later you work toward understanding it.

Drey: This can be done in two ways. One way is to have the active imagination and then try to find out how it relates to life –

von Franz: – try to find out what moves you.

Drey: The other way would be, first, to act out something and then afterwards have an active imagination in order to find out what it is all about.

von Franz: Yes, exactly.

Drey: These are the two possibilities.

von Franz: You can begin at one end or the other, but you must always do both. If you begin with active imagination, you still have to carry out an action; and if you begin with the action, you later have to realize it symbolically. You must always have both realizations. Only then do you have a full realization.

Drey: This is difficult and requires a lot of energy. It is exhausting.

von Franz: Yes it is, I'm sure.

> Another significant analogy is that Kircher conceives his schema as a cycle set in motion by God as the prime cause, and unfolding out of itself, but brought back to God again through the activity of human understanding, so that the end returns once more to the beginning. (par. 418)

Drey: Thus Kircher conceives his schema as a cycle in which the end returns once more to the beginning. What does he mean by "the end returns once more to the beginning"?

von Franz: Well, he thinks in religious terms. The beginning is God and the end is the returning to God. All life comes from God and returns to God. Therefore, this beginning is, for Kircher, who is a Jesuit priest, naturally God. What he means by the word *Monas* is God.

Drey: This means the Self is the secret.

von Franz: Yes.

Drey: God is the secret, because we really do not know what it is. We just experience the image of what it might be.

von Franz: Yes, exactly.

> In this circle, Nature "has related the four qualities to one another and drawn, as it were, an equilateral square, since contraries are bound together by contraries, and enemies by enemies, with the same everlasting bonds." (par. 418)

Drey: Here, Jung has quoted Michael Maier. Now by bonds does Maier mean that mysterious substance?

von Franz: Yes, yes.

Drey: For instance, in the transference which exists between analyst and analysand, it is that psychic energy –

von Franz: Yes, yes. That makes a real bond.

> Maier compares this squaring of the circle to the "homo quadratus," the four-square man, who "remains himself" come weal come woe. (par. 418)

Drey: Maier compares the squaring of the circle to the *homo quadratus*. Would that be the whole man who has developed the four functions to a maximum degree?

von Franz: Yes, the individuated man who has developed the functions to a maximum degree. Correct.

Drey: And the four-square man "who 'remains himself' come weal come woe" means the man who stays in the Self all the time. Is that correct?

von Franz: Exactly.

> The ὄργανον κυκλικόν, the circular apparatus that assists the circular process, is mentioned as early as Olympiodorus. (par. 420)

Drey: Now the *organon kyklikon*: does *kyklikon* lead to the word *Kugel*?

von Franz: Yes, *kyklikon* means "round." *Organon* means "instrument" or in this case "vessel." Thus, a round instrument. For a chemist, a vessel is an instrument, so it means the spheric vessel.

> Dorn is of the opinion that the "circular movement of the Physiochemists" comes from the earth, the lowest element. (par. 420)

Drey: The "circular movement of the Physiochemists comes from the earth," that is to say, from the chthonic feminine. Is that right?

von Franz: Yes.

> I have tried, in this book, to elucidate and amplify the various aspects of the archetype which it is most important for modern man to understand – namely, the archetype of the self. (par. 422)

Drey: In what way is the archetype of the self different from the archetype of the individuation process?

von Franz: I would say that the archetype of the Self is what starts and regulates the process of individuation. And the process of individuation is, as the name says, the process of becoming conscious of the Self. Let us say, for instance, that a child has a vision of God; you can say this is the archetype of the Self. Later in life, the child becomes a great personality and slowly realizes the full meaning of his vision has actualized through the process of individuation. It is a slow process of realizing what has always been there.

Drey: What has driven him all the time.

von Franz: Yes, it is what has driven him all the time.

> That is to say a hypostasis of good and evil as metaphysical entities is inadmissible because it would deprive these terms of meaning. (par. 423)

Drey: What does that mean?

von Franz: This means that, although we speak of the principle of good and the principle of evil, we do not know what they really are. *Per se* they are meaningless, for good and evil can only be experienced within a specific context of life. For instance, you cannot say: faithfulness in marriage is good. Once you examine closer, you find it is not true: it is sometimes true and sometimes not. Therefore if you hypostasize, you are making a general abstract principle out of good and evil, which is absolute nonsense. Good and evil have a meaning only when we say: what you are doing here is good, and what you are doing there is evil. I mean good and evil have a meaning only in terms of a practical human judgment.

Drey: But not as generalities?

von Franz: Not as generalities. If you hypostasize and make an abstract generality out of them such as we have to serve the good – this is just humbug.

> The *coniunctio oppositorum* engaged the speculations of the alchemists in the form of the "Chymical Wedding," and

> those of the cabalists in the form of Tifereth and Malchuth or God and the Shekhinah, not to speak of the marriage of the Lamb. (par. 425)

Drey: Now, in what way is the Lamb or the marriage of the Lamb a *coniunctio oppositorum*?

von Franz: All mystical teachings, the Cabala and so on, have in the final state a mystical marriage. In Christianity, at the end of Revelations, there are strange allusions to the marriage of the Lamb. Now, we know that Christ never married, and therefore never united with the feminine principle or his opposite. But at the end, he marries the Church, which is comprised of the people who have survived. Therefore, there is a union of opposites: between Christ and common humanity, or the Church, which is personified as a female and identified with Mary.

Drey: Where does the Lamb come in?

von Franz: The Lamb is Christ. He is the sacrificed Lamb. He is the Easter Lamb. And if you read Revelations by John, you will see there are strange allusions about the sacrificed Lamb, namely, Christ, that will, in the end, marry. Also in medieval mystical literature we find Christ at the end; he marries his bride, the Church. This signifies a mystical union of mankind with God.

Drey: So Christ is the Lamb, and the marriage of the Lamb is the marriage of Christ to the Church. Is that right?

von Franz: Yes.

*The wording here is from the original edition. In the second edition, this sentence is revised and transposed to paragraph 417.

Claude Drey

CLAUDE DREY, BORN NOVEMBER 13, 1919, was raised in Frankfurt am Main, Germany. His Jewish heritage forced his family to flee the country in 1932. The Drey family initially settled in Milan, where Claude continued his education. They ultimately immigrated to the United States, settling in New York City in 1939.

Claude's interest in psychology began at an early age. His mother, Lily Cramer Drey, a professional graphologist, had studied with Toni Wolff and integrated the disciplines of graphology and psychology. Claude's introduction to psychology was from the Jungian perspective, and he was a voracious reader of Jung's works.

During the 1960s Claude began making annual trips to Zurich to study at the Jung Institute. Unfortunately, his first trip came just after Jung's death, so he never met Jung personally. Over the course of many years, he interviewed both Aniela Jaffé and Marie-Louise von Franz extensively. The interviews focused on interpreting Jung's writings and add significantly to the subject matter. The interviews were taped, but up until now they were not available to the public. With this first-time publication of the Drey–von Franz interview, the reader will find additional insight into Jung's works.

In New York City, Claude became a founding member of the New York Jung Institute. He assisted them in their business development and installed their first computer system. He worked privately with analyst Lenore Fabish, who had trained at the Jung Institute in Switzerland. In later years, he continued his studies with Dr. Nathan Schwartz-Salant.

By profession, Claude Drey was a business man, owner of a water-cooler company. However, he had many other interests which he pursued to professional levels. He was a photographer, a masseur, and, along with his partner Francoise Richards, he led courses in communication for couples. Claude had so many interests that he became known as a Renaissance man. He dedicated his life to the pursuit of knowledge. He was a forceful figure, and his passion and intensity was palpable to all who knew him. Claude touched many lives, and he inspired many to go into the field of psychology.

We are all grateful for his contributions.

Diane Drey
Iris A. Drey, M.D.

Sources

Charles, R. H. 1985. *Apocrypha and Pseudepigrapha of the Old Testament.* London: Oxford University Press.

James, Montague R., trans. 1924. *The Apocryphal New Testament.* London: Oxford University Press.

Jung, C. G. 1938. Psychology and religion. In *CW* 11:3–104. Princeton, N.J.: Princeton University Press, 1958.

_____. 1944. *Psychology and Alchemy. CW*, vol. 12. Princeton, N.J.: Princeton University Press, 1953.

_____. 1946. Psychology of the transference. In *CW* 16:163–326. Princeton, N.J.: Princeton University Press, 1954.

_____. 1948. Symbolik des Geistes. Studien uber psychische Phanomenologie. *Psychologische Abhandlungen* 6. Zürich.

_____. 1949. Über das Selbst. *Eranos-Jahrbuch, Band XVI: Der Mensch.* Zürich: Rhein-Verlag, pp. 285–315.

_____. 1950a. Gestaltungen des Unbewussten. *Psychologishe Abhandlungen* 7. Zürich.

_____. 1950b. Concerning mandala symbolism. In *CW* 9i:355–383. Princeton, N.J.: Princeton University Press, 1968.

_____. 1951. *Aion: Researches into the Phenomenology of the Self. CW*, vol. 9ii. Princeton, N.J.: Princeton University Press, 1959.

_____. 1952a. Answer to Job. In *CW* 11:355–471. Princeton, N.J.: Princeton University Press, 1958.

_____. 1952b. Synchronicity: An acausal connecting principle. In *CW* 8:417–531. Princeton, N.J.: Princeton University Press, 1960.

_____. 1955–1956. *Mysterium Coniunctionis. CW*, vol. 14. Princeton, N.J.: Princeton University Press, 1963.

_____. 1957. The undiscovered self (present and future). In *CW* 10:245–306. Princeton, N.J.: Princeton University Press, 1970.

_____. 1960. *Modern Psychology, Vol. V–VI: Alchemy*. Zürich: Karl Schippert and Co.

Jung, C. G., et al. 1964. *Man and His Symbols*. New York: Doubleday.

Schärf-Kluger, Rivkah. 1967. *Satan in the Old Testament*. Hildegard Nagel, trans. Evanston, Ill.: Northwestern University Press.

von Franz, Marie-Louise. 1949. The "Passio Perpetue." Elizabeth Welsh, trans. *Spring 1949*, pp. 85–127. Republished Irving, Texas: Spring Publications, 1980.

Index

Barbara Hannah was born in England and went to Zurich in the 1920s to study with C. G. Jung. She remained in Switzerland where she was a practicing analyst and teacher at the C. G. Jung Institute. She is the author of *Encounters with the Soul and Jung: His Life and Work, A Biographical Memoir.*

Marie-Louise von Franz, born in Austria, immigrated to Switzerland with her family as a child. She earned a Ph.D. in classical languages from the University of Zurich and became a scholar of ancient Greek and medieval Latin. She met C. G. Jung in 1933 and worked with him until his death in 1961. Her large number of published works include *Alchemy, Number and Time*, *The Grail Legend* (in collaboration with Emma Jung), *On Dreams and Death, C. G. Jung: His Myth in Our Time*, *Psyche and Matter*, and many unsurpassed works on fairy tales.

Claude Drey, born in Germany, immigrated to the United States as a young man. An avid scholar of the works of C. G. Jung, he was a founding member of the New York Jung Institute.

www.ingramcontent.com/pod-product-compliance
Lightning Source LLC
LaVergne TN
LVHW051044220926
848485LV00001BA/2
* 9 7 8 1 6 3 0 5 1 0 4 5 9 *